Opera House
Tottery

Diana

with thanks and best wishes.

Nicc?

Opera House Tottery

Zaha Hadid *and the* Cardiff Bay Project

Nicholas Crickhowell

UNIVERSITY OF WALES PRESS • CARDIFF • 1997

© Nicholas Crickhowell, 1997

British Cataloguing-in-Publication Data.
A catalogue record for this book is available from
the British Library.

ISBN 0-7083-1442-2

Jacket design by Olwen Fowler
Typeset at University of Wales Press
Printed in Great Britain by Cromwell Press, Broughton Gifford, Wiltshire

To Zaha Hadid with admiration for her creativity and skill

and her strength in adversity

Contents

Illustrations

Some of the principal players referred to in the text

Secretaries of State for Heritage and chairmen of the Millennium Commission

The Rt Hon Peter Brooke MP
The Rt Hon Stephen Dorrell MP
The Rt Hon Virginia Bottomley MP
The Rt Hon Chris Smith MP

Other Members of the Millennium Commission

The Rt Hon Michael Heseltine MP   Sir John Hall
Simon Jenkins   Michael Montague
            Jennifer Page, chief executive

Secretaries of State for Wales

Lord Walker of Worcester (formerly   The Rt Hon John Redwood MP
    The Rt Hon Peter Walker MP)   The Rt Hon William Hague MP
The Rt Hon David Hunt MP
            Michael Scholar, Permanent Secretary

The Cardiff Bay Opera House Trust

Lord Crickhowell (formerly
    Nicholas Edwards, Secretary of
    State for Wales), second chairman

Mathew Prichard, formerly chairman
    of the Welsh Arts Council, later
    president of the National Museums
    and Galleries of Wales, first
    chairman of the Trust

Alun Michael MP, deputy chairman
Lord Davies of Llandinam (David
    Davies), chairman of WNO and
    a competition Assessor
Christopher Bettinson
Patrick Deuchar
Sir John Tooley
David Williams, Board member WNO

Wynford J. Evans, deputy chairman
Alun Davies (dec. 1996)
David Richards
Lewis Evans
Sue Harris
Dennis O'Neill
Dame Gwyneth Jones

            Mandy Wix, project director

Welsh National Opera

Lord Davies of Llandinam,
chairman, a Trustee and
competition Assessor
Lady Crickhowell (Ann), Board
member and wife of author

Hugh Hudson-Davies, also CBDC
Board member
David Williams, Trustee and Chairman
of the Friends of WNO
Anthony Freud, director

Lucy Stout, director of development

Cardiff Bay Development Corporation

Sir Geoffrey Inkin, chairman, and for
a time a Board member of WNO

Russell Goodway, leader of South
Glamorgan County Council and
Cardiff County Council
Sir Alan Cox
B. K. Thomas

Lord Brooks of Tremorfa (Jack
Brooks), deputy chairman and a
competition Assessor
Hugh Hudson-Davies, Board
member WNO
Professor Richard Silverman, a
competition Assessor, and chairman
of the CBDC's design and
architectural panel

Barry Lane and Michael Boyce, chief executives

Competition Assessors

Mathew Prichard, chairman and the
first chairman of the Trust
Lord Davies of Llandinam, chairman
of WNO and a Trustee
Lord Palumbo
Professor Francesco Dal Co
David Williams, chairman of
technical advisers and a Trustee

Lord Brooks of Tremorfa, deputy
chairman of the CBDC
Professor Richard Silverman, a
member of the CBDC
Paul Koralek
Michael Wilford
Freddy Watson, observer

Advisers to the Cardiff Bay Opera House Trust

Jan Billington, arts consultant
Huw Williams, solicitor
Alan Lansdell, Bovis
Peter Rogers, development adviser
Derek Sugden, acoustics consultant
Paul Koralek, architect

Stuart Lipton, development adviser
Andrew Brooks, Grosvenor
Waterside
Adrian Ellis, arts consultant and
lottery bid adviser
Henry Drucker, fundraiser

Architects and Designers

Sir Norman Foster
Manfredi Nicoletti

Itsuko Hasegawa
Zaha Hadid

Brian Ma Siy, Office of Zaha Hadid

Millennium Bid Assessors
Richard Pulford, arts
Roger Tomlinson, arts

Bob Stubbs, business plan

The National Museums and Galleries of Wales
Tim Edwards (dec. 31 August 1996),
    president and brother of the author

Dr Colin Ford, director

Arts Council and other players
Lord Gowrie, chairman, Arts Council
    of England
Sir Richard Lloyd Jones, chairman,
    Arts Council of Wales
Emyr Jenkins, director, Arts Council
    of Wales

Sir Keith Stuart, chairman of ABP
Martin Scherer, chairman, Cardiff
    Bay Business Forum
Sue Essex, leader of Cardiff City
    Council

Note
David Hunt, and two Millennium Commissioners, Michael Montague and Patricia
Scotland, QC, were included as life peers in the August 1997 honours list.

Introduction

There are no better men than the best of the Welsh and no worse men than the worst.

Giraldus Cambrensis, twelfth century

There may be those who would prefer that the story that follows should not be told. Sometimes, when things do not work out as planned, it may be sensible to close the book in the hope that all may soon be forgotten. That may be appropriate when only private individuals have been involved and personal interests affected; but it cannot be so when the actions of public organizations cause legitimate hopes to be dashed, taxpayers' money lost and the interests of both private individuals and the general public damaged. The bid for Millennium funds to build a centre for the performing arts in Cardiff involved activity over a period of more than ten years by government and a variety of governmental organizations. Among those who played a role were the Welsh Office, the Welsh Arts Council, the Cardiff Bay Development Corporation, the South Glamorgan County Council, the Cardiff City Council, the Millennium Commission and the Cardiff Bay Opera House Trust. Over £2 million of public money was spent. Significant financial costs were also incurred and damage was suffered by an even larger number of organizations in the private sector. These included The Office of Zaha Hadid and the other members of the design team that she assembled; those who entered what proved to be an abortive architectural competition; Welsh National Opera; Bovis and Associated British Ports who backed the bid with money and personnel; as well as individuals who gave up jobs and risked careers to support what they believed was one of the most significant artistic projects to emerge as a result of the lottery.

The papers of the Cardiff Bay Opera House Trust and the models that it commissioned have been deposited at the National Library of Wales and will be available for public inspection. As the Trust was dependent on public funding all those papers can be called for at any time by the National Audit Office and the Public Accounts Committee. In seeking to write a record of what happened while memories are still fresh I have been largely dependent on those documents and I have quoted from them freely.

The story is told because there should be a record of what happened and what went wrong; but it will be of interest to a wider audience than that concerned with the manner in which public money and public affairs are managed. This was a hugely well-publicized story, it involved a major international architectural competition, a passionate row about the winning design, and an architectural designer whose work and personality have stimulated world-wide interest. This record of what happened describes the problems inherent in the management of a large and complex architectural project and of a bid to a Millennium Commission which followed controversial policies that differed from those followed by the other lottery funders. Welsh National Opera, which perhaps more than any other great international opera company sprang from and serves the musical interests of ordinary people, played a central role in which, absurdly, it was labelled élitist and plunged into an unwanted competition with Welsh rugby. The story involves five Secretaries of State for Wales, three Secretaries of State for National Heritage and a Deputy Prime Minister. The conduct of local politicians in Wales, the members of the Cardiff Bay Development Corporation and the press, all of whom influenced the outcome, is described primarily on the basis of the material which they originated.

I hope that this story will be of interest to those concerned with architecture and the management of great projects; to those who care about opera, music and the arts; to those anxious about the management of lottery funds and celebrating the millennium; to those involved in town planning and urban renewal; to those fascinated by politics and the way in which political decisions are taken; and, perhaps above all, to those who love Wales, many of whom threw themselves passionately into the extraordinary debate about this project.

For those who do not know Cardiff a word of explanation may be needed about the geography of the area and my involvement in it. Cardiff Bay is the name now given to the largely man-made area of water at the mouths of the Taff and Ely Rivers that was created by the construction outwards into the Severn estuary of Cardiff docks at a time when Cardiff was the greatest coal port in the world. It also applies to the land adjacent to it. By the time that I became Secretary of State for Wales in the government formed by Margaret Thatcher in 1979 the original nineteenth-century docks that ran almost from the heart of the city to the sea were derelict, and only the most modern part of the port was still active and making an important contribution to the local economy. The East Moors steelworks, which had occupied a large site close by, had recently been closed, and further to the east premises occupied by the Rover car company were about to be abandoned. A vast area close to the centre of the city was derelict and empty, and the neighbouring housing estates were some of the poorest and most deprived in the city. It was a typical scene of urban decay of the kind to be found in many of the old industrial heartlands of Europe and North America.

By the mid-1980s inward investment and economic recovery had begun to transform the industrial situation in Wales. In 1986 as Secretary of State I had set in motion preliminary work on a scheme to construct a barrage across Cardiff Bay which would remove an extensive area of mudflats and create a large freshwater lake close to the city centre. I had consulted widely about the likely benefits of such a project in terms of urban regeneration and environmental improvement, and had visited cities such as Baltimore where great success had been achieved in bringing life and prosperity back to similar wastelands. I announced the decision of the government to set up an urban development corporation, charged with the task of inner-city regeneration, of the kind that had already begun to achieve considerable success in the docks area of east London, and at the same time made it known that the chairman would be Geoffrey Inkin, a former regular soldier, who had done well as chairman of the Cwmbran Development Corporation and of the Land Authority for Wales. He continued in the latter post throughout the course of this story. The Cardiff Bay Development Corporation took up its responsibilities after I left the Welsh Office and ceased to be a Member of Parliament at the time of the general election in 1987. Despite the world recession, by the early 1990s great progress had been made in clearing the dereliction and with constructing new commercial buildings, housing and recreational development. Work had also begun on the barrage, which had been delayed because of legislative obstacles. The desirability of locating a major public building in the heart of the waterside development was recognized from the start. I had referred to the possibility that it should take the form of a centre for the performing arts at the conference in December 1986 at which I announced my plans for the Development Corporation and the Barrage.

Because the interrelationships between the various bodies involved was to have very significant consequences, the reader needs to understand that in Wales the responsibility for most aspects of central government lies with the Welsh Office, headed by the Secretary of State who is a member of the Cabinet. Among its varied and important duties the Welsh Office is responsible for deciding the level of central-government grant to local authorities and its allocation. It issues guidance on planning policy to local authorities; appeals against planning decisions taken by local authorities are made to the Secretary of State. The chairmen and members of statutory organizations such as the Cardiff Bay Development Corporation are appointed by the Secretary of State, who also decides on the amount of central-government grant that they should receive. At the time when most of the events described in this book were taking place there were two tiers of local government: among the relevant functions of the county council was the provision of strategic planning, traffic, transport and highways, while the city council was the planning authority responsible for taking decisions about planning applications. The CBDC had a specific set of responsibilities designed to achieve the regeneration of the derelict land in south Cardiff. Among its members were representatives of both levels of local government.

After leaving the House of Commons and becoming a life peer that autumn, I was asked by Nicholas Ridley, the Secretary of State for the Environment, to set up and become the chairman of the National Rivers Authority, which was formed at the same time as the privatization of the water industry. However, I also continued to be actively involved in Welsh affairs and became a director of Associated British Ports, the largest landowner in Cardiff Bay, on whose initiative the successful development on the waterside would largely depend. I was also a director of HTV, the independent television company covering Wales and the West, and president of the University of Wales College of Cardiff. I served two terms as a member of the board of Welsh National Opera, and was succeeded on the board by Ann, my much better-qualified wife, who had been a member of the Welsh Arts Council and its music committee, and had founded the Welsh branch of Yehudi Menuhin's charity, Live Music Now!

I owe a particular debt of gratitude to Ann for her patience during the preparation of this book and for helpful suggestions about it. Aileen Oates, my secretary at the time when I was chairman of the Cardiff Bay Opera House Trust, played an indispensable role. I must also thank Adrian Ellis and Mandy Wix for much good advice, and Jan Billington, Adrian's assistant, for reading the text and checking the facts. Bob Skinner, the Trust's public-relations officer, contributed valuable material to the section on the press. Huw Williams of Edwards Geldard, and David Hooper of Biddle & Co. also read the text and made a number of helpful suggestions. I alone bear responsibility for any errors that have escaped detection and for the opinions expressed.

1 *The Dream*

The success of those first appearances in Cardiff and Porthcawl brought a flood of applications to join the chorus from throughout south Wales, some from as far away as Carmarthen. Miners and colliery workers, secretaries and housewives, shop assistants and doctors, solicitors and nurses – anyone with a voice who had ever fancied getting up on a stage and singing grand opera wanted to be part of the new company.

Richard Fawkes, Welsh National Opera

Among the enterprising people who founded Welsh National Opera in a south Wales garage more than fifty years ago there were probably those who looked ahead and dreamed of an opera house in Cardiff. They will have been joined since by thousands of ordinary people who have been thrilled by performances of that great company, or who have travelled long distances to hear heroes like Geraint Evans, Stuart Burrows, Dennis O'Neill and Bryn Terfel, or heroines such as Margaret Price, Gwyneth Jones and Anne Evans. There have been many others over the years, struggling to find the money to travel to London by rail or bus in order to see a musical, who must have wished that there was a large lyric theatre in Wales: all these people would have regarded as absurd the suggestion put about later by ignorant commentators that such ambitions were élitist. As long ago as 1984, the Hoggart report for the Arts Council of Great Britain, which examined the building needs for the future, identified two major priorities: a dance theatre for London and a home for Welsh National Opera in Cardiff. Although the completion of the St David's Hall in 1983 for the first time provided the city with a first-class concert hall, there remained a yawning gap in facilities for lyric performances, which were worse than in almost any comparable city in Britain, and ludicrously inadequate for a music-loving nation. In 1985, during the time when I was Secretary of State for Wales, I agreed with Mathew Prichard, who was then chairman of the Welsh Arts Council, that we would commission two reports, one on the housing of the visual arts in Wales and one on housing the performing arts. A small group, ably chaired by a Coopers and

Lybrand partner, Hugh Hudson-Davies, who was to play a prominent part in this story, produced the report on the visual arts in April 1986 which included the interesting idea that an opera house could be placed within the courtyard of the National Museum, and contained recommendations that led me to conclude that the Welsh Office should finance the construction of new galleries to house the Museum's important collection of pictures.

In January 1986 the Welsh Arts Council, with financial support from the Welsh Office and the Cardiff City Council, decided to proceed with a study, to be prepared by Messrs Carr and Angier, of the feasibility of building and running a centre for the performing arts in Cardiff (which became known within the council as the CPA). In the light of what happened later it is significant that the report on that study refers throughout to a 'centre for the performing arts', and the introduction by the chairman to the report (which was published in September 1986) states specifically that the council was aware that the building could not be viable if an exclusive view was taken of its likely use. This was to be 'a popular entertainment centre suitable for musicals, pantomime and other events with a mass appeal'. The report contained an estimate of the number of weeks that might be allocated to its various uses, and the period of sixteen weeks allocated for performances by Welsh National Opera was identical with the estimate included in the bid to the Millennium Commission a decade later. The study examined the suggestion that the centre might be sited in the area partially enclosed by three sides of the museum, and recommended against it. The Arts Council now decided to commission Carr and Angier to carry out a full feasibility study together with a planning and design brief. These, financed with help from the Welsh Office, the Cardiff City Council and the South Glamorgan County Council, were completed in March 1988. The then Secretary of State for Wales, Peter Walker, helpfully announced that a site would be set aside for the centre within the area under the jurisdiction of the Cardiff Bay Development Corporation, but less helpfully, as later events were to prove, urged that it should be called an opera house.

Back in 1986, when I was still in the Welsh Office, I had decided that the most urgent priority was to provide the money to construct the major extension needed for the National Museum of Wales and the modernization of the existing galleries there. Because of the flexibility provided by the block-grant arrangements for financing Welsh public expenditure, and by making some very modest cuts in other programmes, I was able to create a new expenditure line in the Welsh budget, providing about £5 million a year for the work initially. The total out-turn price proved to be about £23 million. I would have liked to commit similar sums for the centre for the performing arts; but even my first commitment was out of the ordinary for that particular administration, and we were also planning to spend large sums to construct a barrage in Cardiff Bay. The Treasury was sufficiently alarmed to provoke the Prime Minister into a critical examination of my Cardiff plans at a particularly difficult meeting of a Cabinet committee. I had to fight very hard, and it was only because both Geoffrey Howe and the Chancellor, Nigel Lawson, were sympathetic that, after the meeting, we were able to agree a formula that gave me the authority I needed. Clearly the centre for the performing arts would have to wait, but when I announced our intention to set up a Cardiff Bay Development Corporation and build a barrage, I also took the opportunity to suggest that if my successors at the Welsh Office were to maintain the expenditure line that I had created it should be possible to provide the core public-sector funding required for the arts centre once the museum project was completed. I hoped that I had established a foundation on which others could build. Both Peter Walker and David Hunt later made public statements supportive of the principle; and David Hunt firmly established his credentials by providing a generous and life-saving grant to Welsh National Opera.

In December 1990 the CBDC (as the Cardiff Bay Development Corporation is generally known) secured agreement from the Welsh Office to fund more detailed investigations into the feasibility of a new centre. Detailed terms of reference were drawn up, and a Steering Group was established. The Steering Group was chaired by Geoffrey Inkin, as chairman of the CBDC, and was made up of representatives of WNO and the Welsh Arts Council, with Associated British Ports (the landowner), Cardiff City Council and South Glamorgan County Council representatives attending as observers. By that time I had retired from politics and was a board member of Associated British Ports. In that role I attended the steering committee. The WNO and the Welsh Arts Council were represented by their chairmen, David Davies (Lord Davies of

Llandinam) and Mathew Prichard. The group met in the offices of the CBDC, which provided all its services, and Barry Lane (the energetic former major-general who was then chief executive of CBDC) took part in all its discussions.

The work carried out by Geoffrey Inkin's group was extremely thorough; the basic concepts that it produced and the design principles that it adopted were those to which the Cardiff Bay Opera House Trust was later to work almost without alteration. The feasibility study that the group commissioned in the spring of 1991 was carried out by three consultants – Comedia, KPMG Management Consulting and AEA, a specialist arts consultancy founded by Adrian Ellis, who was a former civil servant. Comedia, assisted by quantity surveyors and by the architect Paul Koralek, and drawing on the earlier work by Carr and Angier, drafted capital budgets and an outline brief for the architectural requirements. Paul Koralek, who had now entered the scene, was to play a central role in the developing drama; so, too, would Adrian Ellis of AEA, who in due course took almost every part – as consultant, acting chief executive, adviser, friend and general dogsbody. To him goes much of the credit for what we were to achieve, and none of the blame for the disaster that was to destroy us. His report examined the possible sources of funding for the project and proposed a strategy for securing that funding. KPMG assessed the economic impact of the project on Cardiff Bay, Cardiff and Wales.

The first objective of the study was to establish the optimum size and the wider artistic profile of the proposed Opera House. By now Peter Walker's advice had been taken, and that is what it was called. The name had changed, but the conclusions were the same. There was a strong case for a centre with a 2,000-seat auditorium in terms of artistic provision and civic and national amenity, urban regeneration and tourism. Well over 50 per cent of the programme would consist of musicals and just under 20 per cent productions of opera, with a balance of dance and other entertainment. The out-turn cost, if built within five years, would be £63 million. Not more than a third of this could be raised from the private sector, and that amount only if the public-sector funding was in place first. By this time I was becoming worried and impatient. All this work was taking time, and I knew that within the Welsh Office the mice would be energetically nibbling away at the expenditure line in the budget.

Those with other programmes that they thought important would be arguing that with the completion of the Museum project in sight there was no justification for retaining a planning figure for another arts programme. I pressed the point at the meeting of the Steering Group on 17 October 1991, and the minutes record the conclusion that the 'submission of the Steering Group's Feasibility Study to the Welsh Office should proceed without further delay'. However, it was not until 4 December that Barry Lane wrote to John Craig at the Welsh Office with a submission and a request for a pledge of Welsh Office funding – £5 million for the preparatory work needed over the period 1993–6, and a further £20 million on a contingency basis for the construction of the Opera House, to be called upon only in the event of a successful fund-raising effort from other sources. I wrote to Barry Lane to say that the delay was particularly unfortunate in view of the public-expenditure timetable, as it seemed likely that it was now too late for the matter to receive proper consideration in the context of that year's public-expenditure round.

My own contacts within the Welsh Office confirmed that it was now unlikely that we would obtain the funding on the scale that we required from that source. However, in March 1992 the Secretary of State for Wales, David Hunt, responded to the proposals by commending them; and officials asked for an 'addendum' to the feasibility studies which would outline how the project might be taken forward. Shortly after, in the Conservative Party manifesto for Wales for the May 1992 general election, there was a commitment to seek to develop, in combination with the private sector, an opera house for WNO as part of the Cardiff Bay development. The addendum that David Hunt wanted was prepared under the direction of Adrian Ellis by AEA, and published in January 1993. The addendum recommended the establishment of a separate trust with specific responsibility for carrying out the project; and that recommendation was accepted by the CBDC. At the same time the national lottery was under active consideration. Although the detailed provisions and eligibility criteria were unclear, it became apparent to the Steering Group that large capital projects of a cultural and civic nature, for which there was otherwise little available funding, would probably be the focal point of the legislation. A similar conclusion seems to have been reached with relief by Welsh Office officials who now gave support to the steps being taken in the knowledge that their own budgets might be spared.

The CBDC now did three things: they established a company limited by guarantee with charitable status, the Cardiff Bay Opera House Trust; they adopted proposals that had been developed by the steering committee for a competitive process to select the architect, assisted by an architectural adviser, Paul Koralek, who was a member of CBDC'S design and architectural panel, and a partner of the architectural practice of ABK; and they secured Welsh Office approval to fund the Trust's work on a short-term rolling basis.

The addendum, published in January 1993, had been considered by the Steering Group the previous November. A note by Adrian Ellis for that meeting was prophetic, and brilliantly foresaw the storm clouds that lay in our path. It was prompted by the experience of the Opéra de la Bastille in Paris, which Adrian Ellis told us was not anchored in a generally agreed need, so that reactions to it during the critical phase of planning, funding and construction were determined by emotional responses to the building itself rather than to the purposes the building serves.

> This is a question of balance and degree and if the chosen design is unpopular then a demonstrable purpose is only a partial bulwark against a general ebbing of political support and public funding. However, the presentational dangers of edging CBOH through the competition stage without an early, ringing, shoulder-to-shoulder endorsement or explanation of the rationale for the project by its prospective champions are worth considering. Once the opportunity is lost to explain and win allies for the Opera House outside of − and in advance of − the debate surrounding a specific design, it can never be regained.

We had been warned.

Another paper considered at the same meeting was equally important and prophetic. This one was written by the group's architectural adviser, Paul Koralek. It argued that the best way of selecting an architect was by means of a competition; but acknowledged that competitions can 'lead to disaster'. Again we had been warned. Koralek argued that the most compelling objective must be the achievement of the best possible architectural design for the building, and ultimately the best possible building for the project. However, he acknowledged that the very idea of a 'best possible design' raised questions of judgement, and in the profession there was much debate about whether an architectural competition is a method of choosing a design or an architect. That debate was later to envelop the Trust. Koralek in his paper emphasized a point not understood by many of the later critics of the Hadid design, which is that 'a design submitted in competition and selected as the winning entry does not need to be regarded as sacrosanct and final in all its detail', and that 'a subsequent process of dialogue, review and refinement is not only possible but almost always necessary'. He also made the point that the competition design is important as the basis for selecting the architect, and the competition system gives the client the possibility of a kind of preview, a foretaste of the building that he will get. Any other method of selecting the architect requires the choice to be made before this stage is reached. The competition system allows the choice to be made on the basis of both the organization to be entrusted with the project and the design ideas which they would bring to it. With a public project it was particularly important that the appointment should be based on a fair and thorough procedure, and that this could be seen to be both fair and thorough.

For this project Koralek proposed a two-stage competition, based very largely on a procedure that had been used for the Royal Museum of Scotland, but with a variant used in a competition that had been held shortly before for a convention centre at Nara in Japan. A first, open stage, requiring only outline proposals, would be followed, as at Nara, by a second stage, in which four invited architects would be asked to participate with the four from the open stage. All the entries would be submitted anonymously and the four invited architects would enter the competition's second round on this basis. This would have the advantages of an open competition whilst ensuring the participation of some leading architects in the final competition. The procedure would also allow for a degree of contact between the promoter and the participating architects during the second stage, so that a dialogue could develop. Paul Koralek's advice was accepted by the group and subsequently by the CBDC board. Four architects were invited directly into the second round. Sir Norman Foster, Mario Botta, Rem Koolhaas and Rafael Moneo were chosen. Frank Gehry and Tadao Ando were invited but declined. It was unfortunate that the Steering Group accepted Paul Koralek's suggested short-list almost without debate. It was a subject that required wider advice and much more consideration. The group should have talked to the architects and thought much more carefully about the possible consequences of a particular choice of both the selected four and the assessors. One consequence of the procedure adopted had not been foreseen. A number of prominent architects who might have been expected to enter the competition did not do so, probably because they had taken offence at not being among the selected four or because they believed that the winner had already been pre-selected from among them. It was also decided that a colloquium should be held in Cardiff as an exercise in public and community participation. All these arrangements had thus been recommended and the arrangements for the competition set in motion a considerable time before the Trust itself was formally constituted in June 1993. The nature and scope of the project, the design brief and the form of competition were all decided upon by the Steering Group and the CBDC, both chaired by Geoffrey Inkin, and were inherited by the Trust.

2 The Competition

Therefore, I pray you, lead me to the caskets,
To try my fortune.

William Shakespeare, *The Merchant of Venice*

After the November 1992 meeting of the Steering Group, Geoffrey Inkin wrote to the Secretary of State pointing out the dangers of pressing ahead with the competition as part of the feasibility phase (as had been suggested by officials) without being able to give a commitment that the winning team would receive a commission. He therefore asked for provision in the Welsh Office expenditure projections for the following three years for a total of just over £5 million. He reminded David Hunt, the Secretary of State for Wales at that time, that the offer by Associated British Ports to make the land available was contingent upon a firm commitment to begin construction by late 1995 or early 1996. Adequate assurances were obtained. From that time forward all government funding for the project was channelled through the CBDC and became part of that organization's expenditure programme.

Detailed work now began on preparing the competition brief. The administration of the project was placed initially in the Cardiff Bay Arts Trust (a charity that had been set up at arm's length from the CBDC to advise developers and commission works of public art) under the chairmanship of Mathew Prichard, who was to be the first chairman of the Opera House Trust when it was formally constituted. Mathew Prichard had been an effective and well-liked chairman of the Welsh Arts Council and member of the Arts Council of Great Britain for eight years. An employee of the Booker group, he was responsible for the organizational arrangements for the Booker Prize. He is the grandson of Agatha Christie, and was fortunate, while still a boy at Eton, to be given the rights to *The Mousetrap*, the record-breaking play still running in London; and he has devoted time and energy to the management of the Christie Trusts and to the distribution of substantial funds from that source for a great many charitable causes. He has acquired a notable collection of modern sculptures, some of which stand in the garden of Pwllyrach, the Prichard family home in Glamorgan where my father was born (we are cousins). On the death of my brother Tim in 1996 he succeeded him as president of the National Museums and Galleries of Wales. He has been a principal driving force behind, and generous contributor to, the splendid transformation of the old library in the centre of Cardiff into an arts centre. The first meeting of the Arts Trust was arranged for mid-January 1993, and Mathew Prichard took up his task with characteristic enthusiasm.

The preparation of the brief was a major exercise led by Paul Koralek. It was based on extensive research and discussion with all the interested parties, and the Trust devoted a great deal of time and effort to it. When completed, it received a great deal of praise. Again the objectives were clearly spelled out. The main purpose was to establish a centre for the performing arts, in particular opera, dance, musical theatre and drama (though the use for drama was expected to be only occasional). The recently modernized New Theatre was admirably suited for traditional drama, and the Sherman Theatre for smaller and experimental productions. The second principal objective was to help to revitalize the Inner Harbour area in Cardiff Bay. The main auditorium was to provide between 1,750 and about 1,900 seats, and to have a superb acoustic for opera. The brief set out detailed requirements for every part of the building and specified that the designs must be capable of realization within a budget of £43.25 million at 1994 building costs, exclusive of VAT and also exclusive of loose furniture, fittings and professional fees. The budget included allowances, that later looked inadequate, for 600 car-parking spaces.

Before the second stage of the competition, the budget limit was increased, not because of the parking, but because a complicated discrepancy had been discovered in the brief between net and gross areas. The figure set therefore became £46.5 million. Because the original budget costs were later to be critically compared by the press and others with the larger total figure submitted to the Millennium Commission it is worth emphasizing that the bid figures included professional fees, an inflation allowance to the year 2000, together with an endowment fund to cover any possible operating deficit, the first-year running costs and a substantial endowment for WNO. The capital-cost figure that we had in our minds from that time forward, and to which we succeeded in sticking remarkably well was £46.5 million. We were inclined to put from our minds the addition that would in due course have to be made to that for fees and inflation. In the preparation of the brief, however, there was no neglect of this important issue. At the meeting of the Steering Group in January 1993 there was a vigorous argument with Paul Koralek, led by David Davies on the clause specifying the fees. Koralek wanted to write in the fees basis and specify the rate. Others suggested that the amount should not be specified but left to negotiation. Koralek argued that those who entered the competition should know the basis on which they were to be paid. The total professional fees, including structural, mechanical and electrical engineers and quantity surveyors, allowed for in our Millennium bid amounted to 18 per cent, which was in line with the fees for the rebuilt opera house at Glyndebourne, but this level of fees was later criticized by the Commission.

I am told by those involved with other schemes that the Millennium Commission regards 12 per cent as the acceptable upper limit, a figure apparently based on the advice of Sir John Hall, one of its members. That level of fees may be appropriate for a shopping centre but it certainly is not for an opera house, because of the number of different professional advisers involved. Paul Koralek did not only have strong views about the issue of professional fees; but he also wanted the competition rules to state that the appointment would automatically follow the competition result. In the event, the element of discretion that the Trust was to retain for itself was to prove a key factor in much that was to happen after the announcement of the competition result.

The brief contained an appendix on the acoustics prepared by the Trust's consultant, Derek Sugden. It placed emphasis on theatrical intimacy, intelligibility and quality of sound. The number of seats became a subject of vigorous debate despite the considerable amount of research that had already been conducted on the subject. Almost all that research indicated that if the object was commercial viability there was a need for an auditorium with almost 2,000 seats; the acoustic experts preferred a house with not more than about 1,500 seats. Hugh Hudson-Davies, a former partner of Coopers and Lybrand and a CBDC board member, who had produced the original report 'Housing the Visual Arts in Wales' in 1985, argued with stubborn persistence that on commercial as well as acoustic grounds the smaller number was to be preferred. In the end the Trustees rejected his advice. Events, I think, proved that the Trustees' judgement was right: shortly before the Millennium Commission took its fateful decision, Sir Cameron Mackintosh, who has been responsible for putting on so many of the most successful modern musicals, told me in the bluntest possible terms that, without a 2,000-seat auditorium with characteristics to suit musicals as well as opera, there was no prospect that he would bring his productions to the building. I accordingly instructed the design team to modify the internal design of the auditorium, which was at that stage not yet fully developed, so that 2,000 people could be seated for musicals. However those events were still far in the future.

It would have been more useful if Hugh Hudson-Davies had challenged the requirement for 600 parking spaces. This requirement posed a problem for the architects that none of them succeeded in overcoming in a satisfactory manner, and that indeed was probably incapable of solution at the price specified. Putting a large car park under a large auditorium is bound to be an expensive and wasteful business on almost any site, but particularly when that site is made up of ground straddling old docks; putting the car parking above ground is likely to have significant adverse impacts on the size and appearance of an arts centre. Those of us involved in preparing the brief who had enjoyed the convenience of parking under the National Theatre in London, and WNO representatives who wanted a convenient staff car park, underestimated the difficulties, while the CBDC and local-authority representatives hoped that they could get the Millennium Commission partly to fund their parking for them. As a consequence there was an initial planning requirement for the inclusion of parking. It was a mistake. There was ample ground close by for cheaper and better solutions.

Two other decisions taken at this time had significant repercussions. The first concerned Geoffrey Inkin and me. Michael Scholar, the Welsh Office Permanent Secretary, insisted that neither of us could be trustees because of possible conflicts of interest, mine arising from the fact that the terms on which the land would be made available by ABP, the company of which I was a director, had not been finalized. That meant that we both continued our involvement as 'attendees', joining Trust meetings after any business in which we might have a conflicting interest had been discussed. The second significant event was that, at an early meeting after becoming chairman, Mathew Prichard announced that he intended to use his chairman's prerogative, and, advised by Paul Koralek, would choose the assessors for the competition 'in order to avoid argument among the trustees'. His decision was accepted after minimal discussion, and events had been set in train which were to have profound consequences.

The Assessors chosen were Lord Palumbo, then chairman of the Arts Council of Great Britain; Professor Richard Silverman, head of the Welsh School of Architecture at Cardiff University and chairman of the CBDC's Design and Architectural Review Panel; Michael Wilford, a prominent British architect; Francesco Dal Co, professor of the history of architecture, University of Venice; Paul Koralek, the Trust's architectural adviser; Lord Brooks of Tremorfa (Jack Brooks), the CBDC deputy chairman and former leader of the county council; and David Davies (chairman of WNO), with Mathew Prichard as chairman. Freddy Watson, an employee of Grosvenor Waterside, the local property-owning subsidiary of ABP which owned the site and adjoining properties, was a non-voting observer. The fact that the selection was made in this way by Mathew Prichard, and that he chaired both the panel and the Trust, was probably a mistake, because it placed an unfair burden of responsibility on his shoulders and put him in a difficult position later when violent controversy had to be resolved. The intention was that, by combining the two positions, conflict between Assessors and the Trust would be avoided. That did not turn out to be the case. At the time I was a little irritated that I had not been invited to be an Assessor; but I later realized that it was a wise decision in view of a possible conflict of judgement with my colleagues on the board of ABP. Indeed, even the presence of Freddy Watson as a non-voting observer proved a complication when he chose to make up for his lack of a vote by the strength of his expression of strongly held opinion.

In the period between June 1993 and September 1994, when the final stage of the competition was reached, the membership of the Trust was broadened to include members of the business community, the local political community and the performing-arts community. By the spring of 1994 Mathew Prichard had been joined by Alun Michael, the Labour Member of Parliament for Cardiff South and Penarth and former city councillor who was to become a Minister of

State at the Home Office in the 1997 Labour Government; Councillor Alun Davies, representing the city; David Davies, chairman of WNO; Patrick Deuchar, chief executive of the Albert Hall; David Williams, a WNO Board member and chairman of the Friends of WNO; J. Wynford Evans, chairman of South Wales Electricity plc; County Councillor David Richards; and two of Wales's most distinguished singers, Dame Gwyneth Jones and Dennis O'Neill. Emyr Jenkins, director of the Welsh Arts Council was at this stage secretary of the Trust. David Richards was later to be replaced by Councillor Christopher Bettinson. Not all these members attended every meeting, but many did, and the attendance usually also included Geoffrey Inkin or his CBDC representative; Judi Richards who ran the New Theatre for the city; Matthew Epstein, the American director of WNO, or another representative of WNO; Lucy Stout who had been recruited from the National Theatre as director of development for WNO and the Trust; Freddy Watson and Andrew Brooks of Grosvenor Waterside; as well as Adrian Ellis, and me as an observer. Jack Brooks also put in an appearance from time to time. It was a formidably experienced and well-informed group. After Matthew Epstein left WNO and returned to America, his place was taken by Anthony Freud, who had succeeded him as director.

Although, as the funding body, the CBDC was not represented by a trustee, the presence of its chairman, deputy chairman and sometimes its chief executive ensured its close involvement in every decision taken. It provided the money, received the minutes and detailed accounts of expenditure, and two of its board members were assessors. The day-to-day management of the Trust throughout this period was in the hands of Adrian Ellis and the management consultancy AEA. This shrewd and capable former civil servant had established a formidable and well-justified reputation in the specialist field of arts consultancy. His organization had a very full-time job to do: there were presentations to be made to the local authorities; the site acquisition had to be negotiated; competition procedures planned; future project management options considered; future management and the recruitment of a director prepared for; fund-raising programmes developed; and education projects and activities set in motion to ensure that the project was rooted in the community. Things were hotting up.

In June 1994, Peter Brooke, Secretary of State for National Heritage and the first chairman of the Millennium Commission, delivered a speech about the objectives of the Commission. He challenged people in all corners of the United Kingdom to use imagination and vision in producing schemes that seize the 'once in thirty generations' chance to mark the new millennium in style. He announced that funds would be made available for a small number of major projects of national and regional importance, projects that would probably not otherwise happen, projects likely to be unique in some way which might break new ground in design or function, or make a new contribution to public life. He said, 'Architects must seize the chance to house these projects with the ingenuity and style that Paxton brought to the Crystal Palace.' The overture was over; the curtain was about to go up on the first act of the drama.

Two hundred and sixty-nine submissions had been received by the closing date of the competition the previous April. It had been open to all qualified architects, whether from the United Kingdom or from overseas. In the first three days of the judging process the Assessors reached a consensus that about twenty-five projects were worthy of detailed technical consideration, and these were then examined over the next four days by the teams of technical advisers that met under the chairmanship of David Williams, a trustee. The Assessors then reconvened to consider the short-list in the light of the information provided on acoustics, layout and cost. Only when a consensus had been established on the final four were their identities established. Their professional competence was then considered, and they were informed of their success. The firms whose designs were chosen were those of the Office of Zaha Hadid, Itsuko Hasegawa, Neil Morton Associates (at the second stage linked with the Percy Thomas Partnership) and Manfredi Nicoletti. They joined Mario Botta, Sir Norman Foster, Rem Koolhaas and Rafael Moneo for the second round. The profile of the four short-listed and four selected architectural practices greatly intrigued the professional media, which ensured that interest in the competition was now high. Two criticisms were levelled at the competition at this stage: the 'fast-track' invitation to the famous four had few fans, and one disgruntled entrant thought that the four who came through the long route were so 'politically correct' in terms of geographical distribution, gender and other characteristics as to call into question the anonymity of the competition. However, the overwhelming response, from both disappointed competitors and pundits, was that this had been an exceptionally well-managed and thought-through competition.

The second of three colloquiums was held in mid-June, and all the practices turned up for it, undeterred by a rail strike. I attended that colloquium and, standing over Grosvenor Waterside's model of Cardiff Bay, emphasized the importance of making this a building that invited people in by day and night, and not just for perform-ances, so that it brought life and activity into the Bay. This one face-to-face meeting with the final eight was not enough. The quality of the final competition designs would probably have been higher if there had been more talking, a deeper exchange of ideas and a more determined attempt to enthuse competitors with the importance of the project. It was decided that the third colloquium would be held at the beginning of September in the Coal Exchange in Cardiff, at which the short-listed designs would be displayed and public comment invited just before the final judging took place. At the same time the Trustees agreed that it would be useful to have an extended board meeting at a hotel near Cardiff in which to discuss in an informal manner the challenges presented by the Opera House project. The evening of 11 and morning of 12 September were chosen, at the beginning of the week in which the winner of the architectural competition was to be announced. When we made our plans we did not realize what an extraordinary situation was to develop that weekend.

I was not able to be present at the Coal Exchange colloquium, but I did come specially to Cardiff to examine briefly the entries before the judging. It is hard for an amateur to make a judgement on the basis of a hasty examination of small competition models, and drawings hung on a wall. My first reaction was one of disappoint-ment: there did not seem to be one obvious outstanding winner; some of the entries, indeed, seemed bizarre. Was Rem Koolhaas, for example, playing a joke with his entry? Sir Norman Foster had produced an expensive and very professional model of a building which seemed possible; Manfredi Nicoletti's glass wave caught the eye. I did not pick out Zaha Hadid's design, but her drawings are difficult to interpret even for the professional. I attach names but at this stage the designs were still anonymous. I spoke to Mathew

Prichard on the telephone and found that he shared my disappointment, particularly that the pre-selected famous four had produced such unexciting work. I wished him luck with what was clearly going to be a difficult choice.

At the colloquium a small event occurred that was to have damaging consequences. A representative of the *Western Mail* asked for, and was apparently refused, photographs of the exhibits which the paper wished to publish in advance of the result being announced. On grounds of equity to others and to maintain anonymity, the request was turned down, causing the paper to complain that the colloquium was an inadequate form of consultation. A potential friend had been provoked into dangerous hostility at a critical moment. It was critical because the Assessors' choice was going to be controversial. This was recognized by those involved even before the public storm broke. Adrian Ellis, always a shrewd judge and wise counsellor, was quick to spot the danger, and his views were reinforced by Freddy Watson, who from the outset was intensely hostile to the winning design and critical of the way in which the selection had been made. One of the Assessors, Lord Brooks, was equally unhappy, although – after the decision to choose Hadid had been taken by the Assessors on a majority vote – he had moved, and Mathew Prichard had seconded, a motion on which the decision was made unanimous.

We already had very much in our minds the experience of Sydney, where a beautiful building cost fifteen times the original estimate and does not work well as an opera house. Later that became my own particular obsession. Even at this stage I pressed the point that we should not be committed to any architectural team until we were reasonably confident that they could complete the work on time and to budget. For all these reasons some of us were very concerned that the Assessors had chosen, but not yet announced, a winner; but had not picked runners-up. The need to have runners-up as well as a winner was important because of a legal complication. At the time the competition was running, the UK government had not implemented the EC directive on public services, although the date for implementation had passed. We had received legal advice that the competition rules must none the less comply with the directive as the doctrine of 'direct effect' would apply and make the directive enforceable in the courts. If a winner only was named and later the

Trustees wanted to discard the winning design, they would not be able to select another architect without holding a fresh competition. All these possible problems were being talked of by most of us in the abstract only, because we had not yet seen the winning design. The formal selection of second and third choices should have been made earlier, but it was still not too late to do something about it.

The Assessors were invited down to the Cardiff hotel in which we were assembling for our special board, and after a closed session it was announced that the competition had been won by The Office of Zaha Hadid, and that there were two other commended designs, those of Sir Norman Foster and the Japanese architect Itsuko Hasegawa. The Assessors also decided to change the previous unanimous verdict to one of 'a clear majority'. Manfredi Nicoletti's glass wave, which later won popular support, was not selected. We were already up against one of the shortcomings of the competition system, that the choice has to be made by assessors after an inevitably short technical and cost assessment in which the client is hardly involved.

I had arrived quite early at the hotel with others, and had to sit outside the room where Mathew Prichard presided over a difficult conclave of the Assessors whilst we impatiently awaited the verdict. It was thus only after that meeting was over that I examined Zaha Hadid's model for the first time. Again it was almost certainly an error that the Assessors who had been able to return to Cardiff – Lord Palumbo was waiting beside a telephone in Paris, and Professor Dal Co was not present – met separately in secret conclave. If they had met jointly with the Trustees who were not Assessors, it might at that stage have been possible to come to a choice about which there was a broad measure of agreement. By this time the public was taking a keen and critical interest in the way in which lottery money was to be used, and presentation was likely to prove a decisive factor.

As we examined the drawings, after we had been finally joined by the Assessors, and looked at the small perspex model from a variety of angles, many of us began to recognize the qualities that the judges had seen in it and the potential for its further development. We particularly identified the drama of the view of the great angled auditorium block, but all also felt, even at this first inspection, that we wanted to open out that view and widen the gap between the prow-like forms of the two wings. The interaction between architect and client had begun. The interaction between opposing forces in Cardiff had also started, although perhaps we did not recognize it at the time.

3   The Trustees' Choice

Fierce fiery warriors fight upon the clouds,
In ranks and squadrons and right form of war,
Which drizzled blood upon the Capitol;
The noise of battle hurtled in the air.

William Shakespeare, *Julius Caesar*

While the storm was rolling around us that autumn I was still not a trustee, but my involvement was growing remorselessly. With the Sydney and, more recently, the British Library experiences to guide us, I was anxious that the Trust should have the best possible professional advice about construction costs, and I therefore approached Stuart Lipton, who had a good record of completing large buildings to budget. He had been a highly successful developer until the market turned sour; and I had previously sought his advice about Cardiff Bay during my time at the Welsh Office. He had acted as adviser for the new Glyndebourne, and was also advising Covent Garden about their redevelopment. I met Stuart Lipton in London on 17 October 1994 with Adrian Ellis, and Andrew Brooks of Grosvenor Waterside. Lipton brought with him his colleague from Stanhope Properties, Peter Rogers, a brother of Richard Rogers (now Lord Rogers of Riverside) and an engineer by profession. Peter Rogers was to play a central role in our affairs from now on. Stuart Lipton gave us an immensely valuable introduction into the business of successfully managing a project of this kind. He identified most of the weaknesses of the competition design that would have to be addressed. He recommended the quantity surveyors that we should use, and told us not to ask the architect how much it would cost. 'You will get the answer the architect wants you to have.' He defined the rules that we, the client, would have to lay down; and said that he believed that if we analysed the project properly with the chosen quantity surveyor, the project engineer and the architect, we could discover what we wanted to know within a month. He added the comment that Norman Foster was very professional and easy to work with, and that it would be very difficult to work with a

Japanese architect based in Japan. He rang me next day to warn that there was no time to be lost; the moment to act was now.

As a result of that initiative, within ten days I was in it up to my neck. I had been persuaded to join the team, become the chairman of the Building Subcommittee and, as soon as the land deal could be completed, a trustee. Peter Rogers was also in the quicksand with me, joining us to act as our principal adviser on the building project. I went to see Zaha Hadid and her able chief architect, Brian Ma Siy. I told her that I thought her concept had much merit; but that we had to establish as a matter of urgency whether all our requirements could be met and the building constructed within the cost parameters that had been set. That meant that there had to be a period in which, working together with her team, we went through the scheme bit by bit to see how it might be developed in a way that met our needs and could provide the right foundations for a satisfactory working relationship in the future. I made it clear that I was still uncertain whether it would be possible to build her opera house within our funding limits.

At the meeting of the Opera House Trust on 21 October I reported on these discussions and made my position clear. The winning design deserved priority consideration and the initial assumption that it should succeed. It should be judged as a concept that, with significant changes, had the possibility of producing a set of solutions that were both visually and practically exciting. The Trustees had a clear right – and indeed a duty in certain circumstances – to reject the design on grounds of cost, inability to meet the client's requirements or to develop the concept in a satisfactory manner. All these would provide good reasons for rejection, and reasons which would be much easier to defend than any decision based on a somewhat problematic interpretation of public opinion. I quoted from a published account of the history of the Sydney Opera House,

> The competition was won on the basis of an expert judgement by a jury that lacked hard evidence either of the structural soundness of the design or its eventual cost . . . Jorn Utzon had no previous experience of supervising anything bigger than a medium-sized housing project . . . The problem was exacerbated throughout this long period by the fact that the Executive Committee, a part time body, lacked the necessary resources to evaluate the designs in detail and to provide the proper client role that such a major project needed.

I drew attention as well to an article that had been written for the *Financial Times* by Stuart Lipton, and one sentence in it in particular: many clients 'put insufficient time, effort, and discipline into pre-contract analysis'. All those observations seemed particularly relevant to our situation. I recommended that we should follow the route recommended to us by Stuart Lipton. There was a high risk that Zaha Hadid might fail this examination, and we must therefore begin to test the alternatives, which must include the two designs judged to have significant merit by the Assessors, and possibly one or more from the remaining short-listed eight. The job, which must involve establishing the proper patron-client structure to manage the project, could not be rushed – it was vitally important to get it right. We should explain what we were doing and spell out that it was a priority of the Trustees to avoid any repetition of the Sydney or British Library disasters. The advice was accepted, and it was agreed that we should go forward on this basis.

While initially we were proceeding in the uncomfortable knowledge that, like those responsible for Sydney, we lacked hard evidence about structural soundness and cost, and did not have the resources to evaluate the designs in detail, we knew that we had to obtain that evidence and those resources as quickly as possible. However, the world outside, both architects and general public, were rushing to make dogmatic judgements without any evidence at all, and did not seem particularly anxious to have it. The architects and those who spoke for them were quite as bad as the lay critics, and sometimes even more hysterical. Many of them seemed to have formed the impression that the competition had been held solely for their benefit and that the client counted for nothing. Professor Geoffrey Broadbent, for example, sent letters to me and to the *Guardian* in which he suggested that it was entirely scandalous that the Trustees were prepared to reconsider and perhaps even overturn the results of a competition which had selected a work of genius. Following the rejection of Will Alsop's National Centre for Literature in Swansea 'in a similar, quite outrageous way', 'no architect with the slightest whiff of imagination' was going to enter competitions for buildings in Wales after 'such malpractice', he wrote. *Building Design* reported that the Trust's action in effectively reopening the competition had provoked outrage in the architectural profession. Lee Mallet in the same journal said that the Millennium Commission should withhold funds, and RIBA president Frank Duffy spoke of tragedy and farce. Paul Finch, writing in the *Architect's Journal*, asked, 'What on earth does she [Hadid] have to do to convince the trustees?' and reported that, of the many calls his office had received, all were adamant that a decent competition had been run and that the winning design should be built.

However, all was not entirely harmonious even in the architectural world. Marcus Binney writing in *The Times* supported Nicoletti; and predictably the Prince of Wales's adviser, Colin Amery, wrote a stinging attack in *The Financial Times* on Hadid and 'that small group of international architects who perform largely for each other as a kind of travelling circus – reactionaries, representing the kind of absurd architectural arrogance that the public has long learned to distrust'. That made good copy but it did seem a little remote from the brave and astonishingly forbearing lady and her team who were the subject of so many attacks of this kind from her intemperate critics. I said in my response to Professor Broadbent that I gained the impression that the only people who were approaching the matter in a cool and rational way were the Trustees. Later, he was to offer generous praise for our final choice.

Nearer to home the critics were vociferous, and the tanks were being lined up in an increasingly hostile manner on our lawn. While I had been preparing my paper for the Trustees, a senior board member of the CBDC had been preparing one of similar length for his colleagues. There was hardly any aspect of the design that escaped his assault; and he attacked the principle of asymmetry in architecture with particular venom. 'For me', he wrote, 'as for architects and their patrons through the ages, such forms are awkward, angular, unfitted for their purpose, wasteful of space, full of tension and conflict, illogical, restless and uncomfortable.' He suggested that it would be a dangerous and expensive risk to build the asymmetrical plan; and that the refining of the design that would be required – which in all probability would have to be carried out by her associates – would produce a result that was unlikely to have much remaining impact of the Hadid hand. It would also lack the essential architectural coherence which makes great buldings. History was to prove him wrong. Whatever other judgements may be made of the final design, no reasonable person could suggest that it lacked the impact of Hadid's hand or architectural coherence. She had also resolved all the internal problems that he had identified to the entire satisfaction of the client. The assault, however, did not stop at that. There followed an attack on the architectural team's capacity to deliver, and a homily on UK charity law, with the reminder that it requires trustees to act as prudent men of business. For all these reasons this critic suggested that the CBDC and the Trust should turn from Hadid to the two commended designs. In the Trust we thought that prudent men of business should find out the facts before rushing into judgements. A year later officials of the Millennium Commission told us that the team we had assembled represented the cream of British professionals and that there were no construction problems that could not satisfactorily be resolved!

The board member did not rest his case just on a personal view of the design and a quickly formed judgement of the capacity of the team to get the work done. He also questioned Zaha Hadid's eligibility as a competitor on the grounds that she did not appear to be a registered architect, and pointed out that if she had falsely represented herself as an architect she might have committed a criminal offence under the Architects Registration Act as well as a breach of the competition rules. The suspicion was wholly unfounded. Zaha Hadid had acted with punctilious correctness, and the Trust had already sought legal advice on the issue. The prudent men of business were once again moving at least as fast as their and Zaha Hadid's critics. The entry for the competition had stated that the entry was the work of a design team led by Zaha Hadid, but the entry was signed in the name of Brian Ma Siy who was a registered architect with the Architects Registration Council of the United Kingdom, and he had conducted the correspondence with the Trust. Zaha Hadid was not registered with ARCUK, although she was a prize-winning graduate of a leading architectural school, but in none of the correspondence or in any of the papers relating to the Opera House project did she state, hold out or suggest that the practice was one of architect. The legal advice we received was firm. The Trust and Zaha Hadid had acted perfectly properly.

In November the CBDC received an illustrated presentation from Professor Silverman, himself an assessor, who described in some detail the reasons behind the Assessors' decision to recommend the design by Zaha Hadid. The panel had considered carefully whether or not each short-listed design had achieved an effective balance between the various functions of the building. In the Assessors' view, the winning design scored higher points than others in terms of excellent acoustics, natural ventilation within the accommodation buildings, parking strategy, the informal quality which could best encourage daytime activities within the building, and finally a sense of presence and the ability to bring together the separate parts of the building in a dynamic form.

Lord Brooks, another Assessor, took a different view, emphasizing that the panel had not been entirely united in its decision, which he felt had been unduly influenced by the architect members, who had appeared to favour a particular school of architecture. He backed the Nicoletti design. The CBDC Board decided to advance an interim view, in the hope of maintaining an ongoing dialogue with the Trust; but it was very plainly stated that they had serious reservations on the winning design, and they wanted expenditure at present earmarked for advancing and testing the winning design to be redirected to assessing the costs, functional acceptability and buildability of the designs submitted by Foster, Hasegawa and Nicoletti.

Just before the Building Subcommittee of the Trust held its first meeting on 15 November, I met Geoffrey Inkin to discuss the situation that had now arisen. After the subcommittee met I wrote to him to put on record the understanding that he and I had reached, that there must be no confusion about where responsibility rested, and that it must be for the Trustees to take decisions having weighed up all the factors. The Trust welcomed the suggestion of ongoing dialogue, but challenged head-on the suggestion that money advanced for testing the winning design should be redirected.

We intended to continue with our assessment of the Hadid scheme, but we would also ask three firms of quantity surveyors, in addition to the architect's own, to carry out a rapid costing exercise on all four schemes. At the same time we were asking Stuart Lipton and Peter Rogers to carry out an independent building and design-development appraisal of all four schemes. When we received all this information early in January, we intended, with the assistance of our advisers, to carry out a rapid face-to-face constructive dialogue with the Zaha Hadid team over a two-day period to find out the capacity of that team to respond to the client's requirements for amendments to the brief and for the development of the basic concept. At that stage we expected to be in a position to decide whether or not it would be desirable to proceed with a similar face-to-face appraisal of the other design teams. There were those inside the CBDC and elsewhere who did not like what we had decided, and wanted us to drop Hadid at once. The architects on the other hand cried foul, and their journals wrote angry commentaries on what they regarded as an entirely fresh competition. The Trust was determined to give Hadid the chance she deserved as the winner of the competition, while protecting its own position. Nicoletti had been included in the review, partly in response to public opinion, and partly because of some concern that the technical review of his complicated design at the second stage of the competition had left unanswered questions.

On 23 November we issued a press release which emphasized that the winning design was receiving priority attention, but that in the light of other major capital projects which had gone astray we had a clear duty to do everything possible to reduce the risk. That, however, is to step ahead in a situation in which so many things were happening simultaneously that it was hard to keep control. Fortunately in October we had been joined by Mandy Wix to act as our project director, allowing Adrian Ellis to step back from day-to-day administration and to carry out his proper function as consultant and adviser. Mandy Wix was to prove a tower of strength, with the capacity to keep her head when all about her others were losing theirs. In the months that followed, she and her tiny office team coped admirably with a situation which would have broken many large, established organizations.

A first exhibition of the results of the competition had been held at the National Museum of Wales between 5 and 25 October. This had created enormous interest, particularly as we had invited those attending to submit written comments on postcards which were provided at the exhibition. Nearly 8,000 people visited the exhibition, and the situation that we faced was not helped by the fact that the model of the winning design, which had been commissioned for the exhibition and hurriedly prepared while Zaha Hadid was out of the country lecturing, turned out to be a rather brutal interpretation of her concept. We asked Professor Jeff Griffiths of the School of Mathematics at Cardiff to report on the results of this public consultation. A total of 1,370 replies were received; 991 were specific in expressing a preference, and of these 389 were cast in favour of Foster, 330 for Zaha Hadid, and 214 for Nicoletti. When split votes were added, the proportions were similar. Despite the outcry, despite the excellence of Foster's model and the unsympathetic Hadid model (for which the Trustees developed a particular loathing), it was a pretty open race. Since the winner of the competition had already been announced, there was a natural tendency for a large number of the comments to be about the winning design, and this was reflected by the number in the anti-Hadid category and the almost total absence of similar adverse comments about the other leading designs. There were also a good many pleas to the Assessors to 'change your minds'. There was much praise for the staging of the exhibition, which had been sponsored by Associated British Ports, but doubts were expressed regarding the wisdom of seeking views about the merits of the designs. One respondent, for example, wrote: 'The problem with inviting comments is that most are based on aesthetic first impressions, and not on an understanding of the objectives and design features.' Despite the unsatisfactory model, many respondents were converted after coming to the exhibition, and felt that the photographs that had appeared in the press had not done justice to the winning design.

One important criticism was made, and that was that Hadid's building was incorrectly scaled and would dwarf its neighbours, a point taken up separately by Grosvenor Waterside on behalf of ABP, who had a legitimate concern because of the possible effect on the value of their neighbouring properties. The Trustees started discussions with the local authorities about the possibility of removing half the car parking, and at a very early stage of design revision, necessary because of the need to tighten up the use of space, the Hadid team came up with proposals to remove one whole storey from the building and the awkwardly angled car-park ramp at the rear. These changes had the effect of removing the dominating effect, and substantially met the concerns of ABP. It was an early illustration of the ability of the team to respond to the client's requirements, and of the adaptability of the basic design concept. These were issues covered in the review meetings held in December.

In the mean time a second exhibition was held in London in November at the ITN building. At an early stage Nicoletti had made it clear that he intended to be there, and had offered to come to Cardiff to give a personal presentation. Adrian Ellis had warned in a memorandum that the reception to be held at the exhibition on

21 November would be an exciting occasion and that the air would
be thick with intrigue and speculation. 'Sir Norman Foster will be
there with his team, Nicoletti with his and I have a nightmare vision
of them standing by their models like hot dog salesmen purloining
curious passers-by.' In the event, the occasion was a great success,
and the exhibition looked better in the ITN building than it had in
Cardiff. The editor of *Building Design* told Adrian Ellis that 'any
organization taking an architectural commission this seriously has
got to be doing something right. I would be doing exactly the same.
After all it's their building.' The interest continued to be enormous.
Among those who visited the exhibition were a number of potential
financial backers, the Board of ABP, and the Duke of Kent, a keen
opera lover.

I took the opportunity to have a close look at the Nicoletti design,
and I arranged for Professor Nicoletti to call at my office to discuss
his work. He subsequently provided me with technical and other
material. There were those who later alleged that I bulldozed the
Hadid scheme past my colleagues without proper consideration of
the alternatives. Even if my fellow trustees had been the sort of
people who could be handled in that kind of way, which they were
not, a letter that I wrote to Stuart Lipton on 29 November proves
that my mind was far from made up. I told him that I had met
Nicoletti and that I was not alone

> among the Trustees and their advisers in thinking that if our detailed
> examination of the Hadid proposals was to lead to the conclusion
> that we must seek an alternative, there would be considerable
> attractions in switching to Nicoletti if his ideas are viable both in
> terms of current building costs and of future operating costs.
> Although Nicoletti's design received high technical marks in the
> preliminary work by the assessors, it was eventually rejected, very
> largely because of doubts about its technical feasibility and the costs
> likely to arise from heating and cooling a large glass building of this
> kind. Nicoletti himself addresses these issues in his papers in some
> detail and I was certainly not aware that most of his professional
> team were British with considerable experience of British building
> regulations etc. . . . if, as seems likely, there are still considerable
> doubts about the Hadid scheme by late December, I would like to
> begin to move to detailed study of one of the alternatives before we
> have undertaken the away day session with Hadid. If Nicoletti was to

emerge as a serious runner, it would be nice to have some idea of the balance of pro's and con's that was beginning to emerge quite early in January. Yes, of course we could always fall back on safe sound Foster, except that I think it likely that Foster would substantially have to redesign the building in order to meet the Trustees' requirements. These are some thinking aloud ideas for you to ponder.

Meanwhile the press were having a field day, and by the end of November were much excited by the fact that Nicoletti had been to Cardiff to address the Cardiff Bay Business Forum in an event organized by its chairman, Martin Scherer; and that Foster had accepted an invitation to do the same in November. The Forum, representing the businesses in the Bay, most of them small, had been brought into being with the encouragement of the CBDC so that it could discuss its plans with those who might be most affected. Led by its maverick and unpredictable chairman, it had now spotted the opportunity for fame and influence, and was seeking to take over the public-consultation role from the Trust. All this added to the confusion, particularly as the architects were ignorant of the fact that the Forum's activities were entirely independent of the Trust or the CBDC, and that it was not representative of the wider business community in Cardiff or Wales.

All these pressures had created a crisis of another kind. Mathew Prichard, who had bravely and with a great sense of public spirit borne the responsibility so far, was unwell. His wife and his doctor were quite firm that he must take a break and reduce his public activities. Things came to a head while he was away on holiday in Australia at the end of November. Telephone calls were held with Mathew in Brisbane and I was asked by Geoffrey Inkin, with the support of the Trustees, to take over the chair. Later my wife was to complain that we never thought the matter through and that we failed to recognize the scale of the burden I was being asked to assume. However, she was on the board of WNO and was most anxious to see the company settled into new premises. The pending compulsory purchase of WNO's existing offices and rehearsal rooms in the year 2000 by the CBDC, to enable a new road to be built, hung like a heavy weight above the boardroom table in John Street. It was, she now feels, the beginning of the worst year of our married life. I accepted the challenge, and while still undertaking other major responsibilities including the chairmanship of the National Rivers Authority, I took on this immensely time-consuming unpaid job of chairman of the Trustees in early December. By then the heads of agreement for the land acquisition from ABP had been settled, so that there was now no question of there being a conflict of interest.

We had now begun a process of review that was to take us until February 1995 under the direction of Peter Rogers. That gave plenty of time for the critics to gather their forces and increase their activities. The Secretary of State for Wales, John Redwood, back in October at the Welsh Conservative Conference had been critical of the design and had effectively called for a referendum of the Welsh people to decide the issue, but senior officials in his department were not comfortable at the prospect of the Secretary of State commenting on design issues in a way that might compromise his statutory responsibilities. Others outside the department wished he would extend the practice of consultation to his own decision-making process. Within the Trust Freddy Watson, who was only there as an observer, increasingly intervened in a manner that made a calm appraisal difficult. I was keeping my chairman at ABP, Sir Keith Stuart, and my colleagues on the board fully informed about what was going on, and did not find it easy to have one of our employees taking up a maverick position of his own. It was also personally distressing because Freddy Watson had been one of the civil servants who had thought out the imaginative scheme to build a barrage in Cardiff Bay, and he had played a central role in the successful later development of those ideas. I had been responsible for his recruitment by ABP after he had left the Welsh Office, and I had no desire at all to fall out with him over issues of architectural design. Freddy Watson wrote me a letter on my appointment as chairman urging the early abandonment of Hadid, and he forcefully persisted in his attempts to stop that scheme going forward during the weeks that followed. Sir Keith, who did not personally favour the Hadid design, never attempted to impose his personal judgement on the Trust, and was later responsible for ABP providing substantial sponsorship for the Trust and WNO fund-raising activities. He now decided that it would be better for everyone if Freddy Watson ceased to be directly involved in the project.

Martin Scherer and the Forum were causing even greater chaos. Nicoletti had leapt at the opportunity provided by the invitation from the Forum. A vote of its members, published in their monthly newsletter, showed that he had the support of 55 per cent, which was an indication of just how fickle public opinion could be. It had been Foster who had the largest support among those who had submitted cards at the museum exhibition; but by mid-December Foster, too, had put in an appearance at the Forum and used his considerable marketing powers to advance his case. Foster was openly critical of the selection process, and in particular the lack of opportunity to make a presentation to the Trust.

Freddy Watson, writing yet another letter to me after this event, warned about a backlash if Hadid was pushed through by hook or by crook, and argued against her being allowed to make substantial changes in her winning design or the Trust changing the brief, which he said would be very easily recognized as 'devices to achieve a pre-determined result', leading to accusations that the Trustees had made a mockery of the competition rules and the whole selection process. That was an extraordinary argument because in the same letter he told me that what had been impressive about Foster's presentation was that he had already recognized many of the features in his own design that were causing concern and intended to make substantial changes in it!

Meanwhile other architects, leaders of the profession and journalists were beginning to question the ethics of such appearances, pressures that were shortly to lead Foster into a series of manœuvres that would astonish the Trustees. Other qualified professionals were concerned about what was going on for other reasons. John Lovell, a director of Ove Arup and Partners had written to Martin Scherer after the Nicoletti appearance to express unease about the event and to point out that this was a highly technical building which needed study by experts.

> I think the Forum needs to tread carefully. Without the benefit of expert knowledge, your members may advocate an unviable scheme and lose credibility . . . My view is that costs . . . will progressively rise. All of the competition entries will encounter cost escalation; my guess is that this will be the most expensive of all with the least opportunity for value-engineered cost reductions.

Zaha Hadid also addressed a meeting organized by the Forum, and Hasegawa was brought all the way from Japan for the same purpose.

The Trust was meanwhile getting on with its examination of the winning design, with the aid of its professional advisers. At the Building Committee meeting on 9 December we had received the initial report on the costs of the winning design as a result of a desk-top analysis carried out by quantity surveyors. For the first time I really began to understand how difficult it was to arrive at accurate figures based on the limited information available from competition drawings. However, it seemed clear that the design presented exceeded the brief in area by a large amount. It was little help that much of this additional space was accounted for by the concourse that was one of the most attractive features of the design, providing accommodation as it did for those activities that the Trust was so anxious to encourage within the building. There were substantial discrepancies between the estimates provided by the four quantity surveyors; but the general conclusion was that at this stage the costs could be nearly 50 per cent higher than the limit set, because the building was about 35 per cent over size. However, despite these alarming figures, Peter Rogers, reporting the results of the Stanhope analysis, advised that the Hasegawa and Nicoletti schemes were high-risk and high-cost compared to the Foster and Hadid schemes. Foster was low-cost and low-risk. He believed that the Hadid design was adaptable, but Nicoletti's would require substantial development expenditure, and running and maintenance costs were likely to be high. The Trustees at their meeting the same afternoon agreed that the examination of the Hadid scheme should continue; that informal enquiries should be made about the Nicoletti scheme, with the object of allowing the Nicoletti professionals the opportunity to persuade the Trustees that the fears about development and running costs were not justified; and that Foster was still a possible option. If necessary, full in-depth studies of the alternatives could be carried out once the results of the Hadid examination were known.

A crucial meeting was held with Zaha Hadid at the Architectural Association in Bedford Square on 21 December. It was attended by all her team and our advisers. The object was to examine the robustness of the scheme and the technical issues and points that had been raised by WNO. After much discussion it was agreed that it would be necessary to get 9,000 square metres off the scheme, to relocate the large studios in order to meet WNO requirements, to reduce the bulk of the building and its impact on its neighbours, and to resolve the technical issues. There was also a thorough discussion on the need to meet not only WNO requirements but also those of other companies who would use the auditorium for musicals and similar entertainment. Commenting on the question of scale, Zaha Hadid said that, given a major performing arts centre, it was not unreasonable that it should be large in terms of other development, and that, after all, cities accommodated big and small buildings in proximity. She understood the criticisms about the back of the building, and said that this was an aspect that could be addressed. When Peter Rogers pressed her to give some indication of the kind of solutions that she might be thinking of, she said, 'you are squeezing me like toothpaste.' There was an extended discussion of the technical issues, and when Zaha Hadid said that she was happy to continue those discussions the following day but was reluctant to commit herself to a meeting on 30 December, on the grounds that she could not be expected to redesign the whole project over the holiday period, I told her that I saw the meeting on the 30th as being of fundamental importance, and that while we would not expect her to redesign the building, we would expect to have a clear indication of what her solution to these problems was likely to be. I pointed out that apart from the possible changes in the car-parking requirement, nothing new had been added to the debate that afternoon – all the points raised had been raised repeatedly over recent weeks and I felt sure that she had been putting her creative mind to finding solutions. I told her that if the Trustees were not completely satisfied, they would, following the meeting on the 30th, be bound to enter into parallel exercises with one or more of the other design teams. I made it equally clear that she had been given absolute priority and that we had not conducted face-to-face discussions with others. As clients, we had to be satisfied with the proposals, and if we were not satisfied we would clearly have to seek alternatives. After the meeting had broken up, Peter Rogers told me that he did not think that I had been too severe, and Paul Koralek said that, though he would very much regret it if it did prove necessary to look at other designs, he very much understood the Trustees' position. While all this was going on, the CBDC was pressing us to get on with the equal and parallel examination of Foster and Nicoletti at once.

When I came to report to the Trustees on 6 January I was able to say that very considerable progress had been made despite the fact that Zaha Hadid had spent most of the holiday in bed with a severe bout of flu, and that the seven days between meetings had included Christmas and Boxing Day. The Building Committee had met in Zaha Hadid's office that morning. Among the proposals accepted were the removal of one whole floor in the height of the structure except for the fly tower and auditorium, a change in the angling of the quadrilateral and a tightening of spaces, which had the effect of reducing the excess volume inside the building and of increasing the areas of land on the site outside. The size of the foyers was reduced, alternative arrangements were made for parking, and – particularly welcome – there was a considerable opening up of the views to and from the auditorium. As a result of all this it was judged that we would be much closer to budget.

Equally important, it had been established that significant changes could be made without compromising the concept that had won the competition, and that the architect–client relationship could be made to work creatively. The changes in the parking offered the possibility of some very exciting solutions for the rear façade. Alun Michael was disappointed that these options had not been further developed, but this was not surprising, given the time and resource constraints. Peter Rogers's view, on behalf of Stanhope, was that Zaha Hadid had an interesting scheme that was still inefficient in area terms, but with plenty of scope for further reduction. The scheme was workable. She had shown that her scheme concept was robust enough to meet the original brief and to encompass the new options that were now being considered. The scheme was intrinsically buildable within the required time-scale using existing technology. Zaha Hadid would need strong management and a clear brief. She responded well to challenges and, given a clear and very tight brief, she would produce exciting solutions. She would have to be paired with another architect, because her practice was too small to produce and to manage the volume of work required; but she knew this and would be happy to do it. She already had a strong professional team, and in particular Ove Arup and Partners had extensive design and project-management experience of similar projects of this scale.

If the Trustees turned to Foster he would have to change his scheme substantially, but he would come up with solutions. Nicoletti's problems could not be easily solved. There were serious concerns about development costs, the long-term viability and running costs, and particular concerns about fire risks. Given time and money, a scheme might be developed, but this was unlikely in a cost-time pattern that would not prejudice a Millennium bid.

The Committee put forward its conclusions and recommendations to the Trust at a meeting on 6 January. Zaha Hadid remained a very strong option. She had a concept that could meet a high proportion of the Trustees' needs. She had shown the potential for developing the concept in response to clear demand. She had won the support of the Stanhope team as well as the Assessors. However, on the basis of our advisers' estimates she was still substantially over the stated cost objective. Her designs remained controversial, and, although much improved and showing considerable scope for further improvement, her solution was still likely to provoke substantial opposition. There was a strong demand from the CBDC, local authorities and ABP that the Trustees should consider further alternatives before taking a decision, and the results of the public consultation supported that requirement. The public presentations organized by the Forum had been well attended. It would be hard to explain why the Trustees should be the only people not to listen to the case advanced by the alternative candidates. The Building Committee therefore concluded that the Trustees should now receive presentations; but they judged that because of problems with the Hasegawa design, the difficulty and cost of working with a team based in Japan and the general lack of support for her scheme, Hasegawa should not be invited back.

Sir Norman Foster should be invited and should be asked to cover the concerns of the Trustees, which included the impact of his high and dominating flank wall on Pierhead Street, turning it into a dead end and obscuring the views of the Pierhead Building and the Bay; an awkward pinch point by the Oval Basin; inadequate upper-level foyers; dull street façades; inadequate vehicle-access arrangements; and a number of matters raised by WNO, including the characteristics of the auditorium.

Nicoletti would also be invited and given the opportunity to respond to questions about the extent of the development work that had been done, and to explain technical points about the complex structure. He would be asked whether solutions had been found to the problems connected with ventilation, heating and cooling, and fire; and about maintenance and refurbishment costs. There were serious shortcomings with the buildings beneath the canopy, particularly the narrow gangway exits from the auditorium and the disappointing foyer space on the ground floor. The committee had noted the firm conclusions offered by the Stanhope team that it would be too costly and time-consuming to find solutions, and that though a building on these lines could be developed, it was extremely improbable that it could be done within any budget likely to be available to the Trustees. In the face of this advice and the similar conclusions of the Assessors, Professor Nicoletti and his professionals should be invited to persuade the Trustees that the advice given to them was incorrect.

All this work would have to be paid for; and confirmation would have to be obtained from The Welsh Office and the CBDC that funds would be available. The battle for adequate funding for our own operating costs, the studies of the various designs, and the development work that would be required on the selected design, was ongoing and a constant source of anxiety for the Trust. It was a reason for potential friction with our funders, the CBDC, particularly when we differed on the appropriate course of action.

Money also had to be found for the vital fund-raising activities of Lucy Stout and her development team, who by now were working almost unbelievably long hours. They had the formidable task of raising the substantial sums needed to keep WNO in business at a time when the government was reducing Arts Council funding, while at the same time they set up an organization capable of raising the large capital sums needed if the Opera House was to be built. ABP had come forward with a most helpful offer of up to £500,000 for development funding, but it was made on condition that there was a matching amount from the public sector. The Trustees at the meeting on 6 January 1995, and often at later meetings, spent as much time talking about fund-raising sources as about design. I was greatly helped by the fact that J. Wynford Evans had agreed to take the chair of the Finance Committee and had taken a firm grip on our financial affairs, a task not made easier by the fact that we had had to operate with a part-time treasurer, and by the manner in which the CBDC administered the arrangements that applied under the terms of the financial memorandum.

When the Trustees discussed the Building Committee's recommendations, some argued that we should go boldly for Hadid immediately, despite the implacable opposition of CBDC to the Hadid scheme. Lucy Stout, present as our principal fund-raiser, was one of those who wished for a bold decision, and she stated that the Hadid scheme had already generated great interest and excitement among those able to give generously. The Foster design might not prove a unique enough project for the extraordinary fund-raising required. After vigorous debate it was decided that the examination of Foster and Nicoletti would proceed and that they would be asked to give their presentations on 27 January.

As we moved into this critical phase we strengthened the Trust. Wynford Evans and Alun Michael had been elected deputy chairmen at the meeting the previous December. They formed a Chairman's Committee with me, able to meet between Trust meetings, with the power to take management decisions in a fast-moving situation. We elected Susan Harries, Lewis Evans and Sir John Tooley as trustees. The new deputy chairman, J. Wynford Evans, was chairman of South Wales Electricity and a director of the Bank of Wales. The other deputy chairman, Alun Michael MP, had been a member of Cardiff City Council and of its subcommittee which had acted as client for the building of the St David's Hall. Sue Harris, a free-lance arts consultant, had been head of community and education at Welsh National Opera, where she was responsible for the first two community operas performed in Ely and in Splott within the city. She was responsible, working with Alun Michael, for the development of our important community and education projects. John Tooley, the former general director of the Royal Opera House, Covent Garden, was a director of WNO and chairman of the Almeida Theatre. Lewis Evans, a former regional director and general manager of Lloyds Bank, was managing director of Giro Bank and a director of the Alliance and Leicester Building Society. Taken together, the trustees represented a formidable battery of knowledge and relevant experience. This was one of several meetings when Dame Gwyneth Jones had flown from Zurich to be present and make an expert contribution. Dennis O'Neill was stalwart in his support. Patrick Deuchar, chief executive of the Royal Albert Hall, and David Davies, chairman of Welsh National Opera, who had been trustees from the start, seldom missed meetings in spite of the amount of travel (at their own expense) that attendance involved. David Williams and our local-authority representatives were equally conscientious. At these meetings, when important decisions were being taken, Adrian Ellis, Richard Silverman (our architectural adviser), Judi Richards (manager of the New Theatre), Lucy Stout, and WNO and ABP representatives were all present. Later in the year, as tension with the CBDC increased, Richard Silverman found his double role as a CBDC board member and a Trust adviser too difficult, and he gave up the latter position.

With the decisions taken and the invitations sent, two subsidiary dramas now developed. Martin Scherer became very excited about our decision not to invite Hasegawa, and – after numerous exchanges of views – the Forum offered to pay her expenses. It was decided to accept that offer, and arrangements were made for the architect to travel from Japan.

The second drama was more significant and much more extra-ordinary. Since his appearance in Cardiff in December, Sir Norman Foster had come under increasing pressure from other architects and from the architectural press not to return. Amid pages of letters and comment in the 10 January 1995 edition of *Building Design*, there was a short article reporting that Foster had 'seven days to make up his mind amid calls from the profession that he should decline . . . Foster, who is on holiday, has not yet committed himself.' We did not know Sir Norman's whereabouts, but we were concerned that we could get no response from him. We were told that his office was working flat-out making substantial changes to his original competition entry. He had been due to appear on a panel to discuss architectural competitions at the Royal Society of Arts in London, with Sir Simon Hornby in the chair. He did not turn up. The business or holiday in Spain, if that is where he was, may have been urgent; but perhaps he judged the RSA event one best missed. I was not greatly concerned about that; but we did need to know whether he intended to make a presentation or not. We decided to set a deadline, and told him we must know by close of play – by which we meant 6 p.m. – on Friday 20 January. As we closed the office that Friday there was still no news, but we had reports from his office that his team were still at work.

On the Monday morning I telephoned his office to be told by his secretary that he was holding urgent discussions on the subject at that moment, but would telephone me later in the morning. When eventually he did so, it was to convey an extraordinary message, though not as extraordinary as the letter that was to follow by hand. The gist of the message was that this was a very important project; his was a very great practice; so great a project deserved its skill and experience; but unfortunately he was under very great pressure from his colleagues, and after all Zaha Hadid had won the competition. It was all very difficult and embarrassing. In the circumstances he did not feel free to make a presentation to the Trust, but we were welcome to see the work that his office had been doing on the design. The letter, nearly three pages long, was rambling and diffuse, beginning with a declaration that the proposal was the basis for a dialogue 'which would have produced a world-class building, a landmark symbol, a satisfied user and a final account that would have been within your stated budget'. Sir Norman said that he was 'dismayed to read statements . . . that we have exceeded' the stated budget. This was untrue, and to refute these misleading statements 'it is our intention to counter these by expanding on that subject in a report which will be available to you before Friday'.

There followed a paragraph that was in effect a statement that a new and substantially different design had been prepared:

> We realise that we have addressed many of the design issues raised in your letter. For example by re-evaluating the car parking this makes way for a very generous loading dock. In turn the footprint of the building on the site can be reduced to leave views down Bute Avenue without interruption. More generous breathing space is also created between the Opera house and the Inner Harbour to alleviate what has been described as a 'pinch point' and to create a handsome new plaza. At the Cardiff Business Forum I sketched out an idea showing how you could create a more dynamic and striking roof line by echoing the curve of the glass wall with metal roofs on the other three sides. This, together with the opportunity for dissolving the raking walls into glass, creates further cost benefits. It also produces a more dynamic building.

There followed a reminder that the competition conditions allowed the trustees to move on to the next-placed architect, an attack on the hysteria and hypocrisy of the press, and a criticism of the lack of dialogue in the competition. There was a touching declaration that the project 'is close to our hearts', together with a statement that the appointment of Zaha Hadid would be supported, all leading at last to the conclusion that it would not be 'in the best interests' of the project for the firm to appear in Cardiff the following Friday: 'on balance, we feel we should decline your kind invitation. However this should not be interpreted as this office withdrawing from consideration by the Trust. We will forward a copy of our report – which we believe will be helpful to the Trustees'; and then a nice touch: 'We have no intention of billing you for this work.' Sir Norman issued a statement to the press which said:

> In view of the complications surrounding the Cardiff Bay Opera House competition, Sir Norman Foster and Partners are declining an invitation by the Opera Trust to make a presentation of their proposals on Friday 27 January 1995. However, many misleading statements have been made about the cost of our proposals. To confirm that they met the competition budget, we will be submitting detailed validation on this subject to the Trustees.

Sir Norman was widely praised for his 'withdrawal', and most people assumed that all he would send to the Trustees was a financial validation. Instead Peter Rogers was asked to bring down to Cardiff and to present a large portfolio of drawings of the drastically revised design. It seemed to the Trustees that Sir Norman was trying to eat his cake and have it, and whatever remaining confidence they had in his proposals was effectively destroyed by these events and his letter. Despite this, on 27 January the scheme was conscientiously presented by Peter Rogers in the absence of Sir Norman but failed to impress the Trustees, many of whom felt that it was not an improvement. In a light-hearted aside I made the comment that it looked rather like a mushroom in a field of grass, which prompted a whispered response from a colleague, 'No, much more like a jellyfish coming out of the Bay'. It may have been of some comfort to Sir Norman that Stanhope confirmed that the original scheme had been within the cost plan, and that the original scheme was the closest of all the schemes under consideration to meeting the requirements of the brief. However it was not only the Trustees who seemed to have lost interest in the Foster design: even among the still large army of Hadid opponents it now had very few backers. Sir Norman Foster is a great architect who has produced some very fine buildings; but somehow on this occasion he was not at his best.

4 The Presentations

New opinions are always suspected, and usually opposed, without any other reason but because they are not already common.

John Locke

While we were having these interesting exchanges with Sir Norman Foster, we were also not having an easy time with the CBDC. Hugh Hudson-Davies sent a memorandum to colleagues on the CBDC board on 3 January 1995 praising Foster's design and his presentation of it at the Forum meeting just before Christmas. He expressed every confidence that with further work Foster would produce a world-class design. He said that no such confidence could be placed in Hadid. Foster had a strong in-house core team, used to working together to shared values and standards. No temporary scratch team from different practices – such as Hadid and Arup with their different cultures, values and methods of working – could be an adequate substitute. Looking back on many months of working on an almost daily basis with Hadid's almost 'scratch' team, I can vouch for the fact that Hugh Hudson-Davies was completely wrong in his conclusion; but it was the kind of comment that helped to build up further opposition to Hadid within the CBDC. He finished his memorandum by expressing the

> hope that, after their December meetings with Hadid, CBOHT will conclude that they have at last done enough to satisfy the competition process and that they will now feel free to get on with their real job of securing a world class building for Wales. I hope they will immediately enter into a dialogue with Foster and Nicoletti and they will see, as a hundred Forum members have already done, that the best chance of building a world class opera house is through appointing a world class architect. Failure to do this, in the face of the mounting evidence, would, I suggest be negligent.

That prompted the response he wanted within the CBDC, and on 6 January Geoffey Inkin told me of the board's 'overwhelming opposition to the appointment of Hadid', a situation that he confirmed to me in a letter on the 8th.

> I hope very much that this will not lead to public conflict between the Trust and the Corporation, but should that prove to be so it will trigger similarly vigorous opposition from the Local Authorities, the Bay Business Forum (who have had the most thorough comparative briefing of all) and other representative groups.

I suppose I had to be grateful that the letter at least confirmed that the necessary funding for the next stage would be provided; but the comments led to further sharp exchanges between us over the next few days. In a letter on the 10th I told Inkin that I and my fellow Trustees were astonished and dismayed that the CBDC should have reached the point of expressing 'overwhelming opposition to the appointment of Hadid' at a moment in the process when the Trustees, who were far better informed about the studies that had been taking place, had reached no conclusion themselves about the merits of the schemes. I said that it was 'particularly astonishing and regrettable' that the board should have reached these conclusions, and should be making threatening noises about the consequences, when they were not in possession of the results of the review exercise which had produced substantial design improvements and suggested a number of interesting solutions to some remaining problems. I pointed out that the CBDC had decided on the competition route before the Trust came into existence, but seemed totally unaware of the consequences of that decision; and I noted that while the Trustees might decide to take a different view from the Assessors of the competition, for moral, practical and legal reasons they should only do so after proper process and on adequate grounds. I concluded my letter with an offer to hold a meeting with his board before we took our final decisions; and added that it would be extremely difficult to have a worthwhile discussion if the board insisted on prejudging the outcome and attempted simply to impose its decision on the Trust.

On 11 January Zaha Hadid gave another public presentation in Cardiff which was attended by Inkin but did nothing to soften his hostility. The Competition Scheme Review prepared by Stanhope was presented to the Trustees on 27 January. It commended the original competition brief and concluded that the Office of Zaha Hadid had shown during the course of the review that the scheme concept was robust enough to meet the competition brief and to encompass the new options that were being discussed. Although the scheme had not yet fully met the financial criteria, there was no reason why this could not be achieved. The appointment of the Office of Zaha Hadid was, therefore, recommended subject to certain conditions and with appropriate management procedures in place.

Stanhope told us that the dramatic architectural statement of Manfredi Nicoletti's wave form of roof enclosure, which made that scheme exciting, also made it technically the most complicated. The technical aspects had not been fully thought through, and the scheme represented the highest risk. Independent cost estimates suggested it was about 50 per cent above the allowance in the original competition brief. There were concerns about environmental conditions under the wave; the degree of visibility through the roof, and the likely high maintenance costs. Sir Norman Foster's scheme was, in Stanhope's judgement, the nearest to meeting the technical requirements of the competition brief, including budget. However, perhaps this scheme was the least 'interesting' and the most likely to need radical redesign to give it greater appeal. Foster had the most effective office with the ability to meet the targets, but might be overstretched because of his involvement in numerous other projects. It was Stanhope's initial view that Hasegawa's scheme had many of the problems of the Nicoletti scheme, and that there was inadequate provision for parking.

The report included an analysis of the way the project might be taken forward. The Trustees had also obtained a detailed legal opinion from their solicitors, Edwards Geldard. Huw Williams, a partner in that firm, devoted much time and effort to our cause, and his advice given on a range of questions was invaluable. His advice on this occasion was that, whatever decision we took, one or other aggrieved party might seek to challenge our legal right to make that decision in the courts. As I have already explained, the competition took place in a situation covered by the European Community directive concerning the award of public-sector contracts. This was because the project was to be over 50 per cent publicly funded, lottery money being treated as public money for this purpose. It followed that if the Trust decided that it could not agree a contract with the Office of Zaha Hadid, the decision had to be based on the criteria in the regulation, namely that the contract would not be the most 'commercially advantageous' or that the Office of Zaha Hadid and her team did not meet the criteria concerning financial or technical capacity. The only ground for negotiating directly with Nicoletti, or any other architect other than Hadid, Foster or Hasegawa, without a new selection process, would be that the design was chosen for 'artistic reasons'. This was an element so difficult to define as to run the risk of the Trust being challenged in the courts as to the reasonableness of following that course of action as opposed to starting a new competition process. If we were to make such a choice we would clearly need to take advice from leading counsel.

Thus prepared, the Trustees received presentations from the three architects and Peter Rogers's commentary on the Foster revision over two days on 27 and 30 January. I prepared a detailed summary for the Trustees after the final presentation on the 30th. First I dealt with costs. Since the competition, the four architectural design teams had, with their own quantity surveyors and challenged by our advisers, defined their spaces, reduced excess space and pruned their costs. On a strict competition basis, and with a full number of parking spaces, the four now claimed the following costs, calculated at 1995 prices: Hadid £48 million; Foster £45 million; Nicoletti £55 million; and Hasegawa £56 million. With 300 parking spaces taken out, and other changes that had been discussed, our advisers believed the costs would be: Hadid £46 million; Foster £47 million; Nicoletti £52 million, but with a very significant risk of further cost escalation; and Hasegawa £54 million, also with a significant risk of further development costs. These were basic building costs without fees, contingency, inflation allowance, running costs or endowment. In summary there were two low-cost and low-risk designs and two high-cost and high-risk designs. We had also been given a commentary from WNO, supported by Patrick Deuchar, on the internal arrangements. There were no significant problems not capable of resolution in the schemes of Hadid and Hasegawa. Nicoletti's auditorium and stage were well thought out, but there were significant concerns about ventilation, his foyer spaces appeared totally inadequate and some of the rehearsal spaces were awkwardly placed. There were strong criticisms of the size and positioning of

Foster's foyers, the character of which seemed to have been dictated and constrained by the sloping front of the building. There were very strong criticisms of Foster's auditorium, with its three large overhanging galleries, on both aesthetic and acoustic grounds.

The examination of the teams at the presentations concentrated on structural issues. Hasegawa's design was deliberately centred on the auditorium which she called 'the ship', which was in the centre of a very simple shed-like structure with a sloping anodized-aluminium roof broken by glass lights. The ship had glass walls and an aluminium roof. The double-glazed glass walls with fritting were going to be an expensive feature, and much development work remained to be done to solve the ventilation problems and to meet British fire regulations. The architect was charming, but her English was not good, and her presentation was largely in the hands of a young American assistant. Miss Hasegawa acknowledged problems of communication, but we judged that even pairing with a local architect was likely to be an inadequate solution.

Sir Norman Foster's building, revealed clearly in the drawings sent down, was compact. Its structures were conventional, and its costs within those laid down in the competition, but the anxieties about his auditorium and front-of-house spaces were substantial. Anthony Freud of WNO believed that the auditorium was 'fundamentally not right for opera'. Just as people had different opinions about his original design, which had become widely known in Cardiff as the 'flying saucer', so opinions differed about the very different building which he had now produced. He had replaced the original simple curve on the Oval Basin façade, with its upward-curving lip, with a more complex scallop-shell form. It was rather surprising that, having previously placed much emphasis on the great flank walls, he had now decided that, like the ankles of a Victorian lady, they should be covered with skirts; while his flight of steps, which seemed to echo a pre-Columbian Central American temple, had now also half-disappeared under the same canopy. Like its predecessor it would, if built, have created a gentle, unalarming image of Cardiff, comfortable to live with, but perhaps it would not have been the landmark building that we had been seeking.

Professor Manfredi Nicoletti's team had done a good deal of work since the competition to rationalize and improve the roof structures; and we were advised that these now presented no significant construction problems. Nicoletti confirmed that, unlike Paxton's Crystal Palace which was almost 100 per cent glass, his roof would have been 40 per cent metal and 60 per cent glass, the bottom of the V-shaped gutters being metal and the top of the Vs being made of rectangular fritted-glass panels. Views through the fritted glass of the steeply angled roof and between the metal gutters would have been a good deal obscured; but though it would not have been quite the transparent glass wave that many people imagined, no doubt the fritting could have been reduced at key points to improve the views. The striking warped wall at the rear of the building was to be constructed of 50 per cent metal and 50 per cent glass in alternate panels, standing at right angles to each other, so that the view would have moved from a clear outlook in one direction to a completely blank wall as anyone inside the building turned to look towards the north-west and the city. It was confirmed that this warped wall might have had to be substantially modified to reduce its high cost. The cleaning costs would certainly have been higher than on a conventional building; and although the gaskets between the glass and other vulnerable joints were to be covered with carefully selected materials, Nicoletti's consultant confirmed that there would be an ongoing maintenance need with some significant replacements about every twenty years. It was reasonable that we should be anxious about this kind of thing.

The Sydney Opera House had to undergo major refurbishment and tile replacement at a cost of A$20 million in the early 1990s; and the Pompidou Centre in Paris faces closure for two years from 1997 for similar reasons.

The major problems, however, with the proposed structures were environmental. In theory air (and smoke) were to be extracted by wind entering through louvres at the top of the building. However, when I pressed the architect on the point, he had to admit that this might not work if the wind was from a generally northerly direction and if the louvre control system broke down during a fire. It was even more doubtful that a natural ventilation system would have extracted smoke. The consultant admitted that these were all worrying points requiring further study, and that it would probably be necessary to fit extractors on the top of the warped wall. It was not at all clear how easy it would be to provide the conditions required for different activities all taking place under the same roof.

There were other problems identified about meeting fire regulations within the building. The conclusion of our advisers was that these structural and environmental problems could probably be overcome, but that they represented a significant risk in terms of time and cost. There would also have had to be substantial redesign within the building to overcome the inadequacy of the lateral spaces around the auditorium, and other problems relating to the management of people within the public spaces.

Zaha Hadid, ably assisted as usual by Brian Ma Siy and by her professionals, put forward a clear presentation of the alterations that we had discussed on 30 December, and produced effective drawings of the design changes and the options for the rear of the building. She also described how the public spaces within the courtyard would be landscaped for a number of different uses, with gardens and areas for outdoor performances. We received suggestions from her consultants on adjustments to minimize any adverse wind effects. The team had also done a good deal of work on traffic and access issues.

Each of the presentations was impressive in its own way; and the Trustees and others present inevitably formed different judgements about the range of complex issues examined, and will have reacted differently on the subject of architectural style. It seemed clear that they all had positive virtues, and that none deserved the degree of hysterical hostility that the design of the unfortunate Zaha Hadid had received from otherwise sane and sober people. With the presentations complete, I gave a report to CBDC members and local-authority and Forum members on 3 February.

Alun Michael was generous in his praise of my command of the complex brief, but felt that I had been too critical of Nicoletti. However, my colleagues were fully capable of forming their own views and expressing them. For example, Andrew Brooks of Grosvenor Waterside, acting as our project co-ordinator, made it clear that he had been more impressed than I had by Nicoletti's presentation on the technical problems. He thought that the internal layout beneath the wave, which seemed to me to be a bit of a mess, represented cost-effective grouping, and he praised the parking arrangements. He rightly drew attention to the fact that the Hasegawa presentation had suffered from the unfortunate late withdrawal of Ove Arup from her team, and, despite concern about bulk and cost, believed that with further development the scheme could transform into a very attractive landmark. He was very critical of the Stanhope conclusion that Hadid had succeeded in getting her costs down to our budget limits, and he continued to be worried about the possible wind-tunnel effect that had always been a source of anxiety to those familiar with weather conditions in Cardiff Bay. The fear was that the strong prevailing south-west wind off the Bristol Channel would funnel under the wings and through the open mouth of Zaha Hadid's courtyard creating uncomfortable conditions for visitors within and making open-air performances impossible. Alun Michael was also about to produce a detailed paper setting out the case for Nicoletti in an effective way. From outside we had lengthy documents from the Forum, letters and comment from the chairman of the CBDC, a cascade of mail, and a barrage of press comment. In short, the advocates as well as the witnesses had presented all the relevant arguments comprehensively and well. The jury was about to withdraw to consider its verdict; but before it did so there were to be some last-minute attempts to nobble it.

On 4 February I reported the conclusions of the review to the public in a full-page article in the *Western Mail*. I took the opportunity to remind people of our objectives, and that this was a once-in-a-lifetime opportunity.

> We are trying to build a music theatre, not just for our great opera company Welsh National Opera but as a home for musicals – why should Welsh men and women have to go out of Wales to enjoy Lloyd Webber or other favourites? – for dance and for the large-scale lyric and theatrical performances.

I also emphasized the importance we attached to community and educational activities. I drew attention to the world-wide interest in the drama, and suggested that if we threw away this opportunity we would be the laughing-stock of many, and would put off others from investing in Welsh projects in the future.

At the meeting on 3 February, Brian Thomas, a local business man and member of the CBDC board, asserted that the Trustees had made up their minds and that I was determined to force through a decision in favour of Hadid, whatever the views of others. That was a bit rich, coming from an organization whose expression of views seemed to represent minds that had been prejudiced and closed from the outset. I reacted very sharply. I told the meeting that I regarded the suggestion as offensive, that it was wholly untrue, that the Trustees had not yet sat down to debate the issue, and that I did not know what their conclusion would be. It was bad enough that in the light of that explicit denial the accusation was soon to be repeated in a letter from Geoffrey Inkin; but, much worse than that, it was also made by the Permanent Secretary, Michael Scholar, in the presence of the Secretary of State in the Welsh Office in Whitehall. I thought it as well to give John Redwood an account of where we had got to and where we proposed to go, and therefore asked for a meeting. Sitting at my old desk, he decided on this occasion to play it cool and to leave most of the talking to his Permanent Secretary. Despite the fact that during the same week a Welsh Office official wrote to a distinguished international singer to say that it would be inappropriate for the department to become involved in any way, Michael Scholar tried to apply the heaviest possible pressure on me to move against Hadid. Once again I was confronted with the charge that I was seeking to bulldoze through a particular decision. On this occasion I was extremely angry and reminded him in sharp terms that, unlike his Secretary of State silently observing the scene from his desk, I was not in a position to take autocratic decisions, but had to deal with a particularly strong body of Trustees, whose final decision I would faithfully represent, whatever it might be. The later history of the project may well have been adversely influenced by attitudes such as these within the Welsh Office, even after the departure of John Redwood.

5 The Appointment

Things were moving to a climax and the tanks were still on my lawn. On 8 February 1995 I received an astonishing letter from Geoffrey Inkin (signed on his behalf by Michael Boyce, the former chief executive of the South Glamorgan County Council, who had succeeded Barry Lane as chief executive of the CBDC in the summer of 1993) in which he asserted that the Trustees 'are determined to select Hadid, without serious consideration of other options'. It was a repeat of the allegation made by Brian Thomas after the presentation on 3 February which I had firmly rebutted at the time, and made again by Michael Scholar at the meeting with him and the Secretary of State in Whitehall, to which I had taken such violent exception. What in reality we were seeing from all these people was an absolute determination that, whatever our judgement as to the merits of the various options, Hadid should not be selected. It was an attempt to exercise power without responsibility, a practice that in other circumstances a British Prime Minister had described as 'the prerogative of the harlot down the ages'. While none of these important people could appropriately be described in quite such rough terms, their attempt to bully rather than persuade was not acceptable. It would be the Trustees, not these others, who would have the financial and legal responsibility of building the selected design on time and within budget, and of managing it as an efficient and cost-effective lyric theatre. I wrote immediately to Geoffrey Inkin protesting at this 'serious, and indeed probably libellous allegation' and his use of the word 'disingenuous', with its clear implication that the Trust was lacking in candour. I reminded him of the specific assurance I had given on the previous Friday, 3 February, that the Trustees had not reached a conclusion and had not even had a preliminary discussion as to what that conclusion might be, and described the events that had followed.

> After the presentations on Friday, the Trustees met at about 4 p.m. and for the very first time I asked those present to give their reaction to the information that they had been given so far. I made it clear that we were not taking a decision; not all the Trustees were present or had been consulted, and we still expected to have further comments from the CBDC and others. The Trustees, one by one, gave their preliminary views. Six of them stated that their position had changed during the course of the immensely careful examination of all the options that we had undertaken, thus giving an effective rebuttal to the offensive suggestion that no serious consideration had been given to the other options. During the whole of the debate I refrained from expressing any view at all, believing that my job as Chairman at that moment was to discover as precisely as I could the views of my colleagues. I thought I might get away without expressing a judgement at all; but, as he left the room to catch the London train, Patrick Deuchar paused and said: 'I think we should know Nick's view'. I then said that I agreed with the majority.

By the time I wrote my letter to Inkin, the Trustees had received from Alun Michael a very detailed and powerfully argued case for making a choice other than Hadid. It was the sort of case that one might have expected to receive from the CBDC, rather than the set of assertions contained in the Inkin letter. I concluded my reply by telling him that we intended to meet the following Friday to take our decision, and I copied the letter to Michael Scholar at the Welsh Office. At that stage I still assumed that we would be receiving from the CBDC before Friday a letter setting out in some detail the points that the Corporation considered particularly important. All we knew was that a majority of the board members were hostile to Hadid and said that they wanted to appoint a 'world-class architect' and build a 'landmark building', whatever that might mean. In the absence of any such letter or any clarification of the board's position we decided to make one more attempt to see if we could find some common ground, or at least some explanation of where individual members stood. We suggested that the chairman and any CBDC members who might be free to do so should meet the Trustees at 10.15 on the Friday for about half an hour before we sat down to take our final decision. When we did gather in the offices of the CBDC, the meeting, which a majority of CBDC members attended, took a good deal longer than half an hour. There was curiously little clarification about which design we should choose except that, in the view of CBDC members, it must not be Hadid. The hostility to her design and the virulence with which it was expressed shocked the Trustees, and caused a number of them carefully to rethink their positions. There was less said about the positive merits of alternative designs and virtually nothing in rebuttal of the risks and unresolved technical problems implicit in a choice of Nicoletti's glass wave. One consequence of these exchanges was that they provoked a debate and re-examination of all the arguments at the Trustees' meeting that followed, which was even more intense than it might otherwise have been.

In any event we had two papers before us that might have been designed to stimulate debate. The first was a letter from Alun Davies, a councillor representing the City of Cardiff. In the light of the events that were to follow, his letter had particular significance, and later – before his untimely death – I obtained his permission to publicize its contents. Living as he did in Ely, and with many years of service on the council, his claim to represent the views of Cardiff citizens was a good deal stronger than that of some from outside the boundaries of the city and of relative newcomers to the business, who claimed the authority to interpret or even dictate what the city was supposed to think. On this occasion, because of work commitments, he was unable to be with us, but he had spoken first at our preliminary discussion the week before. In his letter he referred to the presentations by the architects, or in the case of Foster his representative, and made this comment: 'I do not think that I would have warmed to Sir Norman Foster's designs even if he had presented his revised scheme to us in person. It was neat, but unspectacular and a poor fourth in my view for reasons I need hardly enlarge on here.' He then referred to the fact that Hasegawa had been his initial favourite, but reached the conclusion that though her auditorium still appealed to him, he had grave doubts about the rest of the complex, its costs and accessibility. He had similar doubts concerning the costs and viability of Nicoletti's wave, and judged it to be 'a gimmicky risk that might rapidly become a liability to the Trust's successors during the first decade of the next century'. He came down firmly in favour of Hadid, and confirmed that 'as a trustee that represents the City of Cardiff', he had consulted a good cross-section of the community. Civic colleagues had assured him that the city would support any one of the four schemes, the same assurance that had previously been given us by Councillor Sue Essex, the leader of the Cardiff City Council and chair of the Planning Committee.

The contrary view had been put in a letter from Martin Scherer, on behalf of the group of businesses in the immediate locality that were members of the Cardiff Bay Business Forum, and in a much more formidable and significant manner in the paper by Alun Michael which he presented to his fellow trustees. Alun Michael summarized the discussion the previous Friday which had been 'open, helpful and constructive'; there was general agreement regarding Foster and Hasegawa. The only point on which he disagreed with the presentation that I had given to each of the groups and in my *Western Mail* article was that 'it too easily dismisses Nicoletti'. He elaborated on his reasons in a dozen carefully argued pages of support for the Crystal Wave, 'the most dramatic building', which had 'commanded both professional and public interest'.

When we gathered round the crowded table in our Cardiff Bay office, Alun Michael led the discussion, critical of Hadid but supportive of Nicoletti. The next four to speak were split each way, all agreeing that Foster and Hasegawa were out of the running: Councillor Chris Bettinson, representing the county council, was for Nicoletti. This was an interesting opening; the representatives of local government were divided and Nicoletti was leading three to two. I began to ponder what I would say at the press conference that was to follow our meeting. As chairman I would of course come down firmly behind the majority view, but I was uncomfortably aware that if Nicoletti was favoured we would be unable to announce him as a clear winner, and probably would be obliged to hold a fresh competitive selection process to comply with European law and the relevant UK regulations. Before the meeting we had agreed that we would ignore that fact in making our choice, however great the difficulties it might create, and if necessary go through whatever further process was required.

Among the trustees who spoke next, one confessed to being shaken by the strength of feeling among the local-authority representatives on the CBDC, and several expressed anxieties about risking another Sydney if we chose Nicoletti – in other words an exciting building costing many times the original estimates and not working well as an opera house. There seemed to be a majority for Hadid. At the end of this first round of discussion, which I likened to a Second Reading debate in Parliament about the principle of what was proposed, everyone had had the opportunity to express a view and hear the arguments of others. I had not stated my opinion. It was now agreed that we should go round the table in the reverse direction, each person formally casting a vote. This time the discussion was much shorter, and Hadid was the winner by two to one without my vote. Once again I was not required to express a view.

Everyone agreed that, with the choice made, they would firmly support the decision of the majority. In the weeks that followed, none did so more loyally than my deputy chairman, Alun Michael.

At a crowded press conference in the Cardiff City Hall, we told the world what we had decided. Later the charge was to be frequently made that we never made it clear that we were building a multi-purpose lyric theatre and not just an opera house. The press conference was one of the innumerable occasions when we emphasized the range of functions. The press statement that we issued also drew attention to the fact that the Trustees had to base their judgement on a wide range of factors, and not just on their instincts about its external appearance. It acknowledged a fact not understood, and therefore almost always ignored by the public, that the client–architect relationship was only just beginning. It is no criticism of Zaha Hadid's brilliant original concept that its layout and appearance were to be substantially altered and greatly improved by that process. It was a marriage of often strong-willed partners who grew to trust and admire each other; and like many successful marriages it was to have its stormy moments. Our statement was also part of an ongoing process of attempting to gather public support behind us, and to counter the hostility that had been whipped up by opponents of the scheme in the press and elsewhere.

As we left the City Hall after the press conference, Mandy Wix and I met Martin Scherer. During the course of our decision meeting he had telephoned to say that, having given us the views of the Business Forum, he wanted us to know that he would support whatever decision we took. Now, in the street outside the City Hall, he repeated that undertaking. Two days later he wrote a letter to Zaha Hadid on Cardiff Bay Business Forum paper that was generous:

> May we join the many congratulations you will have received. The winner wins through! Yours may not have been the first choice of our members, but no-one can deny that it is a striking and grand design.
>
> In time people will grow to love it . . . I think it is a great pity that the choice of design got mixed up with a feeling of Londoners forcing their choice on the people of Wales. I have always thought that had the Trust taken the time to inform people, then they could have taken this decision and reached the same conclusions . . . Often after strong battles people come to like each other even more than if they had never had it. I think the debate will have increased the probability that the people of Wales will come to feel it is theirs.

I had telephoned Zaha Hadid before our press conference, and the next day she wrote me a warm and appreciative letter. It was the start of yet another hectic period of activity for us all.

6   Zaha Hadid

The British think contemporary architecture is so definitive and abstract. They're used to a domestic scale. In this country you don't have an abundance of incredible modern buildings, they don't surround you like New York or Chicago. They have never allowed the geometry of the new to filter into the city.

Zaha Hadid, interview in *International Herald Tribune*, March 1995

Who was this Zaha Hadid who had won against the odds and displayed such courage and patience during a severe professional examination and in the face of sometimes vicious public criticism? She is a formidable personality in both character and appearance. She was born in Baghdad, attended university in Beirut, and in her twenties had studied architecture at the Architectural Association in London, winning the Diploma Prize in 1977. She then became a member of the Office for Metropolitan Architecture, began teaching at the Architectural Association with her OMA collaborators Rem Koolhaas and Elia Zengelis, and later set up her own studio at the Association. Her academic and research work developed from that early work in London, and she has been a visiting professor at Columbia and Harvard Universities. She has held master classes and lectured in other colleges and universities around the world. At the time of the Cardiff competition she held the Kenzo Tange chair at the Graduate School of Design at Harvard.

Her growing academic reputation in the 1980s, not just as an architectural designer but across a much wider field of design, embracing urban planning, interiors and furniture, was enhanced by her success in a number of major international competitions. Her first major triumph in 1983 was for a design for The Peak in Hong Kong. This success was followed by first-place awards for competitions in Kurfürstendamm, Berlin (1986), and for an art and media centre in Düsseldorf (1989), a project which won the Erich Schelling prize for architecture in 1994. Her design for an apartment in Eaton Place in London was awarded the Architectural Design Gold Medal in 1982. Much more recently she has been the joint winner of the Living Bridges Competition at the Royal Academy in London. Among numerous other projects, in 1990 she completed the exhibition pavilion for video art in Groningen and in 1992 the installation of the Great Utopia Exhibition at the Guggenheim Museum in New York. Perhaps her best-known and most controversial commission was for the Vitra fire station in Weil am Rhein. Zaha Hadid's paintings and drawings, which she has employed as a medium and for testing her exploration of design, have been widely exhibited, and her work is included in the permanent collections at the Museum of Modern Art in New York, the Deutsche Architektur Museum in Frankfurt and the Getty Centre in Los Angeles.

It is curious, in the light of these successes, how the amateur architects of Cardiff snapped and sneered, and dismissed her as someone whose only building was a fire station; but more relevant was the manner in which those who had commissioned her were generous in their praise. This was well illustrated by a curious episode during the height of the Cardiff row when Geoffrey Inkin slipped away to Weil am Rhein to see the Vitra building, and returned with his hostility apparently confirmed. However, the owner of the Vitra building, on hearing of the visit, immediately telephoned Zaha Hadid and expressed his entire satisfaction with the building that he had commissioned.

The loyalty of her clients is shared by her students and in generous measure by the staff of the small practice that she heads in London. Fiercely determined to defend a design and the principles that underlie it, she can be harshly critical of the compromises that technical requirements or the demands of clients may dictate. While she was diplomatic enough almost invariably to refrain from taking up too bellicose a position with the Trust, even when she clearly felt that we were wrong, she got rid of her irritation by letting fly at the always patient Brian Ma Siy and her design team for the changes that they had devised or agreed in her absence. Despite the metaphorical bruises they suffered in these not infrequent episodes, and the long hours that they worked, her team very obviously found that the experience of collaborating with her was an inspiration and an ample reward. Temperamental and strong willed though she may be, she has a remarkable ability to create team spirit and a totally harmonious search for solutions, not just among her own employees but with all those other professionals, architects, engineers, acousticians, theatre designers and model-makers, who become involved in a major project.

At the start we knew none of this and we often saw her tense and on edge. Like others, we sometimes found the presentation of her ideas, both verbal and through her drawings, hard to understand without repetition and interpretation. Fortunately in Brian Ma Siy she had found the perfect interpreter, who admirably reflected her ideas in his own work and in discussion. Peter Rogers, who like the rest of us only came to know her in the most testing circumstances, observed in his report to the Trustees that she responds well to challenges. Despite the defence of her principles to which I have alluded, she also responds well to the suggestions of her clients, represented in our case by that small group of trustees who worked with her on the detail of the project. Confronted with a proposal or criticism, she might initially dig in her heels; but even when she appeared to be at her most stubborn she always listened and, with remarkable skill, at the crucial moment would come up with an often brilliant solution to what had appeared an intractable problem. If she has a weakness it is in her refusal to understand the wisdom of providing the ordinary public with the kind of impressions that they can understand and which they receive almost as a matter of course from other architects. Those agreeable fantasies with which the populists beguile us, and of which those translucent impressions of the so-called Glass Wave of Manfredi Nicoletti are perfect examples, are not acceptable to Hadid. She resists the bushy trees and hurrying figures that sometimes disguise a harsher reality, and persists with her own beautiful but obscure presentations of truth. Alun Michael and Patrick Deuchar, given the task of obtaining from her the kind of images that were needed if the design was to be sold to a wider public, found it hard going; but in this as in other matters, after an argument Zaha Hadid did what was necessary.

Hadid's experiments with design had sometimes in the past led her down false paths to produce results that will not, I suspect, survive the test of time. It would be astonishing if such challenging and imaginative experiments were always successful. However, the same experiments had taught her possible ways of using shape, colour and finish to marvellous effect. Perhaps those who saw the early models of the Opera House, usually viewed from an aerial perspective, may be forgiven for their mistaken belief that this building was going to look like any other office block, although there are few office blocks which have such thrilling prow-like shapes. Those of us who were engaged on the detailed consideration of finishes and the preparation of the final model were to learn how false a judgement that was, and to discover what dramatic effects she can create by these means.

Again, though we hardly knew it when we started, we soon learned of the depth of thought given by Zaha Hadid to the basic concept and the underlying principles of a design. It was because those principles were firmly anchored in sound analysis that the original competition design for Cardiff proved so robust and adaptable. Later, when it was all over and those who had been so hostile to the project came forward with their own, they made the extraordinary assertion that theirs would be different because, unlike Hadid's, it was designed from the inside out. I can think of very few other buildings that have been so carefully structured on an understanding of its objectives and of what was going to happen inside it. There was something else about this remarkable woman that we did not know when we started, and that was her astonishing strength in adversity and the warmth of her character. These were the qualities that we were about to discover as we plunged together into the maelstrom of activity that was required if the design concept was to be developed and our bid ready for the Commission.

7 Preparing the Bid

When we mean to build,
We first survey the plot, then draw the model;
And when we see the figure of the house,
Then must we rate the cost of the erection,
Which if we find outweighs ability,
What do we then but draw anew the model
In fewer offices, or at last desist
To build at all? Much more, in this great work –
Which is almost to pluck a kingdom down,
And set another up – should we survey,
The plot of situation and the model,
Consent upon a sure foundation,
Question surveyors, know our own estate,
How able such a work to undergo,
To weigh against his opposite; or else
We fortify in paper and in figures,
Using the names of men instead of men,
Like one that draws the model of a house
Beyond his powers to build it; who, half-through,
Gives o'er, and leaves his part-created cost
A naked subject to the weeping clouds,
And waste for churlish winter's tyranny.

William Shakespeare, *Henry IV, Part 2*

The period between the appointment of the architect in early February 1995 and the submission of our initial bid at the end of April was as hectic as anything that had gone before. In the first two weeks we were establishing contractual arrangements in consultation with our professional advisers, and receiving papers on procurement, and debating in particular whether we should go down the construction-management route, and if so with whom. We had to decide on the extent of the design development that was desirable and could be afforded before our bid went in and before we knew whether its initial reception was favourable. There was the urgent need to obtain improved presentational drawings. There was work under way on the very important access and education programme.

We had already appointed headhunters and started the time-consuming and difficult job of trying to find a suitable chief executive. This particular task faced us with a considerable set of problems. In a way we needed two different people: someone with the experience and ability to carry a large and complex construction project to completion; and someone else capable of managing a major receiving house. We decided that we would have to combine these roles, and that we should concentrate primarily on those with senior management positions in receiving houses. We were confident that we could put together a project-management team fully capable of completing the building on time and to budget. We did not overlook the possibility that we might find someone with general management experience outside these fields of activity with the capacity to do the job. The primary problem was that no first-class manager was going to undertake a commitment to the project until there was certainty that it would receive Millennium backing; there was also a natural reluctance by established theatre managers to put their heads above the parapet in a way that might endanger their existing positions. That meant that a small group of us had to spend an inordinate amount of time networking and having extremely private meetings with a number of possible candidates, including one brought for interview from the far side of the world. Perhaps it was not their fault in these circumstances, but, despite the high reputation of our headhunters, they produced a disappointing list, and on the whole we did better with our own contacts. Later in the year we held formal interviews with a number of candidates but decided not to make an appointment. We continued the search, and by the autumn I had met a number of top-grade people who had expressed firm interest in the job if the project received the necessary backing. The time spent on the exercise was not wasted, because I received valuable advice about the project and the future management of the arts centre from a number of people at the summit of the profession.

At the end of February we had cleared another significant hurdle. On 22 February we had given a presentation in London to the Royal Fine Arts Commission. Zaha Hadid and Brian Ma Siy, who spoke after my introductory remarks and responded to many detailed questions, were in particularly good form. Geoffrey Inkin, representing the CBDC, seemed uncomfortable, speaking positively enough about the need for the building, but with obvious lack of enthusiasm about the design. From our point of view, the outcome could not have been better. The Commission endorsed 'enthusiastically the appointment of Zaha Hadid and her office as the designer of the Cardiff Bay Opera House'. It considered that the design was stimulating and inspiring, and believed that the building had the potential to become a worthy landmark for the start of the next millennium. It commended the courage and imagination of the Trustees in choosing the design, and congratulated the Cardiff Bay Development Corporation for its foresight and courageous decision to support the Trustees 'in their choice. Those congratulations probably caused irritation rather than pleasure in the Corporation's boardroom.

At the end of February the Trustees and WNO decided to strengthen previous informal arrangements and establish a joint fund-raising organization under the direction of Lucy Stout, assisted by Henry Drucker, who had created Oxford Philanthropic in January 1994 and since 1987 had been director of development at Oxford University. He had been responsible for launching and managing Campaign for Oxford, which at that time had raised over £280 million from more than 16,000 donors. Lucy Stout had worked for five years for the Association for Business Sponsorship of the Arts (ABSA) She had moved in 1988 to the Royal National Theatre and had become director of development there in 1989. Under her direction the level of private-sector income attracted had grown from £370,000 to just over £2 million per annum. In the autumn of 1993 she had joined Welsh National Opera as director of development with a particular brief to raise the private-sector funding for the new opera house. She quickly created an immensely capable and hard-working team with Julie Edwards and Tracey Ogden.

A joint committee of the Opera House Trust and WNO was established to supervise the work of the fund-raising team and to set ground rules for the distribution of the funds raised between the two bodies. We were all conscious of the fact that we had to ensure that WNO was adequately funded to maintain its high standards, while simultaneously we raised the very large sums needed to build the Opera House. It had already been decided that, in addition to the capital fund required for the construction, we should seek to establish an endowment fund to cover any possible operating deficit, and a separate endowment for WNO to give them financial stability over this difficult period. These were challenging objectives, but we were confident that we could meet them. Once again, as with the appointment of a chief executive, we were confronted with the difficulty that people were likely to hold back until the Commission had declared itself, while it seemed that the Commission would want to see proof of our fund-raising powers before taking a decision. It was a classic chicken-and-egg situation.

At the Trust meeting on Friday 31 March 1995 Henry Drucker suggested that we should find a better name for the building. It was agreed that the matter should be on the agenda for the next meeting; but that in the mean time we should stick to the existing name. It was the start of a debate that was to continue into the autumn. Looking back, I am sure that we took the wrong decision and that, trusting that political sixth sense that had so often guided me successfully in the past, I should have used the ultimate threat of a refusal to go on in order to get the change which I, like Henry Drucker, wanted. By August I was firmly of the view that something must be done, and I discussed the possibilities with Adrian Ellis. On 14 August he sent me a memorandum agreeing that a change was overdue, but suggesting that if it was mishandled it would create as many problems as it solved. He pressed an idea that had been made some time earlier by his assistant, Jan Billington, that we should get the *Western Mail* to sponsor a competition to find a new name. This would have the merit of getting over a message to the community and to the Commission, without doing anything expensive or disruptive in the short term. There were problems in making a change: the name recognition of the Cardiff Bay Opera House was astonishingly high in the UK and abroad; if we changed it at a stroke with no continuity we would simply move from fame or infamy to complete anonymity, which would produce another set of problems – not least in fund-raising. Our logo, all our posters and our literature were Opera House-based. I agreed that these were real difficulties, but people did not understand what was going to happen in the building despite our almost daily explanations.

I found that usually well-informed opera lovers were worried that we would not be able to find enough people to fill the seats in so large a building, to be used as they thought only for opera; others, including those who hate opera, seemed equally ignorant of the theatre's purpose, and expressed astonishment on being told that it was for musicals, dance and other lyric performances as well. On 16 August I sent a fax message to the Trustees recommending that it should be called the Millennium Theatre for Wales, and giving my reasons. I proposed that we should discuss the change at an away day we intended to hold at the Royal Albert Hall in September. We did discuss it then, but for a variety of reasons, and particularly because it was felt that the timing was wrong, I found myself in a minority of one, and the proposal was defeated. But that was far ahead.

Long before that we had suddenly been confronted with the fact that there was to be a Millennium bid by the Welsh Rugby Union, strongly supported by local-authority members in Cardiff, for a new national stadium in the city. Already there was excited talk of it being a competition between stadium and opera house; and – if that was the reality – this was a much stronger threat to our own bid than one that was also running in parallel for a botanic garden in west Wales. If that was bad news, there was better news on a front on which we had previously suffered a terrible battering, the coverage by the local press. We had been working hard on public relations, and Alun Michael had been particularly active. Between February and September we held a series of public presentations. On the very day that the WRU threw its hat in the ring the *South Wales Echo* published a leader declaring that the debate about design should now be over. The time had come, it said, for

everyone who has any pride in Wales to back the capital's own opera house. To knock the opera house is to knock Cardiff. And to knock Cardiff is to shoot ourselves in the foot. The opera house will create jobs, attract visitors and provide a fantastic facility which can be used by people from all over the region. The commission will turn down the opera house if it feels the bid does not have the support of the people of South Wales. It is now up to us.

The *Western Mail* could not yet bring itself to like the design; but it, too, declared that 'an opera house is vital to Wales', and lamented the fact that it seemed unlikely that we could get both rugby ground and opera house.

We decided this was the opportune moment to relaunch the project at a press conference in Cardiff on 18 April 1995. There, in the Norwegian Church where the second symposium had been held

before the competition, we presented the new images that we had
been working so hard to get out of Zaha Hadid. We explained that
although detailed design work could not begin until after the
Millennium Commission's decision, the architect and her design
team had already developed imaginative ideas to ensure that the
building would provide a first-class entertainment venue for Cardiff
and for the world. Alun Michael said that the new images confirmed
that it would look magnificent and would be a world-class showcase
for opera, major musicals and dance. The first of the new images
appeared on the front page of the *South Wales Echo* on 18 April
above the headline NEW LOOK FOR OPERA HOUSE and above a
detailed description of the changes. Inside there were pages devoted
to a photograph of Zaha Hadid, a number of other sketches of the
building and further information about what was happening.

The *Western Mail's* view that it had to be either the Opera House
or the rugby ground but not both was, in our judgement, wrong.
Later, we obtained repeated assurances from Virginia Bottomley,
who that summer took over as National Heritage Secretary of State
and chairman of the Commission, that each project would be judged
on its merits. That, however, would have been dull stuff for the press,
who love a competition and ran this one with unhelpful enthusiasm.
The people of Wales were urged to take sides, and the correspondence columns were filled with partisan letters. Opinion polls were
organized, and not surprisingly more people voted for rugby than for
opera. In the circumstances we thought it remarkable that 26 per cent
said that if they had to choose they wanted the Opera House. We
were careful not to engage in these exchanges. If we said anything, it
was to the effect that we hoped both applications would succeed. My
own personal opinion, shared, I know, by a good many others, was
that Wales needed an improved national stadium, but I was sceptical
that the scheme proposed was the best solution, even in the modified
form that emerged after a first-phase rejection by the Commission.

It always seemed to me that the WRU would have been wiser either
to choose a scheme that had already been prepared to modernize the
existing ground, or to build a new ground on a greenfield site. From
the start I was also concerned that it would not be possible to
complete the chosen elaborate and expensive scheme in time for the
World Cup in 1999. Quite early in the proceedings I asked my
colleague on the Board of HTV, Gerald Davies (the former Welsh

International) what would happen if it was not ready. 'Oh, Nick, we will have to have the Welsh World Cup at Twickenham!' The really bizarre feature of the whole affair was that while the citizens of Cardiff and the amateur architects of the CBDC were having hysterics about Zaha Hadid's proposed building down in the Bay, and the *Western Mail* was complaining about inadequate consultation, this vast project in the heart of Cardiff went forward without anyone outside the narrow circle of its backers being allowed to see the design. Fortunately the illustrations that were published in the newspapers of several unimaginably hideous structures proved to be only ideas that in the event did not survive. No doubt Cardiff will wake up one day to discover what it is that has been built on the banks of the Taff in the very heart of the city, and hopefully will find that it is no more or less of an eyesore than any other large sports stadium.

As we prepared our initial bid we sought letters of support from representative organizations in Wales. Sir Richard Lloyd Jones, chairman of the Arts Council of Wales and former Permanent Secretary at the Welsh Office, had written to Stephen Dorrell who was then chairman of the Millennium Commission on 1 March, making it clear that it was a prime concern of the Council that Wales should be provided with a centre for the performing arts in which large-scale productions could be presented effectively and economically. The letter was unmistakably that of a former civil servant, carefully not endorsing the design in detail, but saying that it had no reason to question the judgement of the Trustees. I would have liked to see it go more directly to the heart of the matter, but that was not in the nature of this lovable and very able man. In my time at the Welsh Office when, first as Deputy Secretary and then as Permanent Secretary, he had been my adviser, he had produced a number of particularly pungent and effective minutes which analysed complex situations with great clarity and proposed realistic solutions.

The letter to the Millennium Commission did say very clearly that the Arts Council of Wales would expect to support an application to the Millennium Fund when the time came. When in April we asked for a short letter to accompany our application Richard Lloyd Jones confirmed the Council's desire that the Opera House should be built. It would have been odd if it had been otherwise, as the genesis of the whole project had been their own report, and the Council had been members of the Steering Group that had prepared the ground for the Trust. Later in the autumn Jennifer Page, the chief executive of the Millennium Commission, was to alarm us and irritate Emyr Jenkins, director of the Council, by wrongly suggesting that the Arts Council of Wales was not firmly behind us.

On 24 April we submitted five copies of our formal application for funding from the Commission. The total capital cost of the project given in our application form was £86.82 million at 1995 prices. The total building costs were at our original target of £46.5 million, to which had to be added fees at 18 per cent, a 10 per cent contingency, fittings and site purchase: with pre-opening running costs of £6.27 million that took the total to £69.82 million. We also included in the total capital costs a £5 million bridge fund for WNO and a £12 million endowment fund to cover any revenue deficit the new centre might incur.

To understand the full implications of what was to happen later, it is worth pausing to consider these figures. The Millennium Commission – and Michael Heseltine in particular – were later to argue that the project was rejected because the costs were too high; but those costs, which hardly altered in total, were in our original application. While there was an increase in the development cost, partly for parking, there was an offsetting reduction in the endowment required following further examination of the operating costs. The numbers were known to the Commission throughout the period when they appeared to favour the project; and at no time during the detailed discussions that were to take place between April and December did anyone in the Commission suggest to us that it would be necessary to reduce the scale of the project if it was to have any chance of success. We were instructed to make our application at 1995 prices, and on a number of occasions we asked how inflation was to be dealt with, and in particular whether the Commission's grants would be similarly adjusted. We never received a response.

Just before the Commission announced its decision it stopped talking about 1995 prices and adjusted our costs by an inflation factor. That inflation increase was always going to happen, and should have surprised nobody. The Commission also criticized the level of professional fees, but at 18 per cent these were a little less than at Glyndebourne, and again had been in our application from the start. We did know from the outset that there was a potential problem arising from the policy of the Commission, which differed from the other lottery funding bodies, of only offering grants of 50 per cent of capital costs, excluding endowment. However, the Commission always knew that we needed £50 million, or 66 per cent of the total required.

As the Arts Assessors, Richard Pulford and Roger Tomlinson, and the Trustees pointed out at the time, the Arts Councils were funding up to 75 per cent of capital projects. Ironically, the Millennium Commission, which had put a marker down that it wished to consider the project, and which later refused to agree to the proposal that, like Salford, it should be jointly funded with Arts Council participation, was placing it at a severe disadvantage compared with large arts projects in England. The difference in total potential lottery funding (allowing for inflation) was about £20 million. This was an issue which was to be the subject of fierce correspondence between Virginia Bottomley, Michael Heseltine and me; it was also to be the subject of a detailed critical report by John Mathews for the Institute of Welsh Affairs. We had no alternative but to go to the Commission, because the Arts Council of Wales received a share of lottery funds related to the population of Wales that was only a small fraction required for a project on this scale. At the time we put in our application we did not believe that we and the people of Wales could really be the victims of such a gross injustice. We innocently went forward on the assumption that equity would prevail, and that the Commission would be open with us and positive in a search for solutions. How wrong we were.

We expected to receive the verdict of the Commission on our application in September. We intended to review specific aspects of the original brief during May and June, develop the concept design to meet the new brief in July, and move into the full and costly design phase in September, coinciding with the first receipt of grant. We became increasingly concerned about the time-scale if the work was to be completed in time for the building to open in the year 2000, and about the problems that we faced in keeping our design team together if work in earnest could not begin very soon. In May we pressed the CBDC to provide the finance to enable us to bring the work programme forward by three months and commission immediate design and development work to begin in June. In early

June we received a welcome offer of help from Bovis as a result of discussions that had been taking place about the possibility of their being involved in the construction management of the project, a role they had performed with great success at Glyndebourne.

We were very anxious by now to be in a position to progress the scheme to the RIBA Plan of Work Stage C, by September, as it was now clear that this was going to be a requirement of the Commission. Indeed at one stage they pressed us to take it to Stage D, but they backed away from that impossible demand on being told that it could cost £2.5 million. Their policy throughout was that the Trust should raise and risk large sums to provide certainty, but that the Commission should risk nothing. In marked contrast to this negative approach, Bovis, like ABP, were prepared to risk their own money. They now offered £250,000 without receiving any commitment that they would get the contract, but on the understanding that if we secured Millennium funding the loan would be repaid without interest. The balance of the £400,000 we needed was provided by the CBDC on a similar understanding that it would be repaid if we were successful. During these negotiations about money Geoffrey Inkin was at his most helpful and positive; and somehow, despite resistance at times from some of his board members, he – with the added help of organizations like Bovis and ABP – kept us in funds to the end.

We had taken legal advice and decided that, to conform to a strict interpretation of EU regulations and previous practice, we would seek tenders for the construction-management post, limiting the eligible applicants to those who had direct relevant experience in analogous projects, who were also able to field a team and provide logistical support of the highest calibre. The advertisement in the *Official Journal* also specified that there had to be a willingness to pre-fund up to £250,000 of work which would be at risk unless the Millennium Commission grant was given. Bovis had that experience and most of their Glyndebourne team, and they won the contract. With the funding now available and the contract managers in place we were able to press ahead.

The decision to speed up the design programme meant that we also had to speed up the revision of the brief, which had previously been planned for August and September. It was now essential to have at the very least some major guidelines ready by early August. Adrian Ellis brought in a specialist firm, Inter Consult Culture, to assist with this work. Charlotte Nassim, its principal, was knowledgeable, strong-willed and occasionally erratic. At times our brief revision meetings required all my skills as a chairman to keep temperaments under control and the ship on course. There is no doubt that though the process was sometimes rather painful, Charlotte Nassim's challenging manner produced in the end notable improvements in the brief. She was not the only person to raise fundamental issues in a challenging way. Inevitably these challenges produced conflicts of view and interest that had to be resolved. For example, while WNO vigorously defined the changes in the internal design that they considered important if the building was to work for opera, David Staples of Theatre Projects Consultants produced a strong paper in mid-May identifying the changes required if the building, and particularly the auditorium, was to be suitable for large-scale musicals. Later there were to be vigorous arguments about such matters as the suitability of an asymmetrical auditorium and the shape and size of the pit. The final report was based on these stimulating discussions and interviews that had taken place, among others, with WNO management and staff, Carlo Rizzi (the musical director of WNO), representatives of Cameron Mackintosh Productions and Apollo, staff of Ove Arup and Theatre Projects Consultants, together with Stanhope and the architectural team. The final version was not ready until early November, but the key guidelines were agreed at meetings in August. Alun Michael, Patrick Deuchar, Sue Harris and I were all deeply involved in this work, which imposed yet more burdens on Mandy Wix and her small team in Cardiff.

Many people seemed to have had the quite incorrect impression that there was a large administrative organization moving the project forward. This was far from the case: an uncertain future and shortage of funds prevented us from making adequate staffing arrangements. There were only two full-time staff: Mandy Wix as project manager and Gill Sims-Williams as co-ordinator. Mandy Wix had been an assistant technical director with Welsh National Opera and administrative director of Diversions, the excellent Welsh contemporary dance company, and had managed many festivals and arts initiatives in Wales since 1973. Gill Sims-Williams had worked as administrator of the Drama Association of Wales, representing large numbers of amateur arts groups, and had also spent time with a number of London PR agencies. This small team was supplemented by part-timers: Michael Clay for a time managed the finances before Elizabeth Cory (with many years' experience at Price Waterhouse) joined us as finance manager, and Bob Skinner (after a career in local government) handled public relations.

In mid-May we heard from the Millennium Commission that they expected to conclude their initial review of applications by early June, when we would be informed whether our project had been selected for second-stage appraisal. We had to keep continually alert to any signals from within the Commission. While we would have preferred to deal with the Arts Councils, whose staff and members had a much clearer understanding of our kind of project and seemed to be much more willing and positive in their efforts to assist applicants, that gate was closed to us for the financial reasons that I have described. Heather Wilkinson, who was then acting director of the Commission, had written to Jo Weston, the lottery director of the Arts Council of Wales, the previous October to say that as a normal rule it did not wish to fund projects that fell within the scope of other lottery distributors, but, in the case of the Cardiff Bay Opera House 'the scale of Lottery Funds it requires would put it beyond the means of the Arts Council of Wales.' It would therefore be ready to consider an application to fund that project. She also said that the Commission had decided that it did not wish to fund applications jointly with other lottery distributors, a crucially significant rule it was to ignore in the case of Salford, and rescind in the case of Cardiff when it was too late for the Hadid scheme.

We heard from a good source in May that Michael Heseltine had made his first appearance at the Commission and, on hearing from other Commissioners that urban regeneration might not be an appropriate object of their fund, had talked very strongly about jobs, and insisted that such projects should be favoured. It was judged that this was a good omen; after all ours was a project that would create jobs, and Michael Heseltine was Welsh and keen on the arts. We decided to do more work on the economic studies and to prepare the material for our application for European (ERDF) funds. We asked Coopers and Lybrand to prepare a case. We also redoubled our efforts to rally public support. Jennifer Page, the Commission's chief executive, was making almost daily statements that this was a necessary condition.

On 14 June we heard that we were over the next hurdle, as were the rugby stadium and the botanic garden. The next stage would include a technical assessment and a visit by commissioners. In our press statement welcoming the news, I referred to the scale of the challenge, and said it involved one of the most ambitious fund-raising campaigns ever seen in Britain. I asked for wholehearted support and said that now was the time for key individuals, funders and businesses to come forward and involve themselves in winning the project for Wales. Anthony Freud and Dennis O'Neill joined in on behalf of WNO. In Salford a similar appeal went out over the signature of the chief executive of the city council. It was sad that such leadership was missing in Cardiff.

We were given ten days' notice of the first visit to be made on behalf of the Commission on 26 June. It was to be represented on this occasion by Jennifer Page, Heather Wilkinson, David Baird and an external technical assessor. We arranged that I would lead a presentation in the Cardiff Bay Visitor Centre where there was a large model of the Bay area and the site. Standing by the model, Geoffey Inkin would speak about urban regeneration and tourism, Alun Michael about our Access and Participation programme, and Chris Bettinson and Alun Davies on behalf of the county and city councils. Moving to a conference room, our specialist teams would deal with fund-raising, the WNO, project development and the design. We would then visit the site and a Grosvenor Waterside model of the area in the Pier Head building. In addition to our own people we invited the director of planning and the senior planning officer of the city to be present. It was a formula that we were broadly to repeat for subsequent visits. As far as we could judge all went well and we had covered the ground effectively.

Other Commission visits followed in quick succession, the first from Michael Montague on 29 June. He was met by Mandy Wix, Adrian Ellis, Lucy Stout and Peter Rogers. Alun Michael and I were to have a lengthy discussion with him later in London. On this first visit he said that he was an enthusiastic supporter of the proposal and had spoken out vigorously for the project in all Millennium Commission meetings, and that it was his firm view that the project should happen. However, the key issues were: Where was the matching funding? Where was the private-sector support? Where were the local authorities? Where was the Welsh Office? Our representatives explained the difficulty of generating funding without a much firmer commitment from the Commission. Montague was sympathetic and talked of drafting a Millennium Commission letter which would commit the Commission to funding if matching funding was produced, thus helping to galvanize other funders. It was a concept that got short shrift from officials, although it was the kind of thing, impossible for us, that suddenly became possible when Michael Heseltine wanted support for the Millennium exhibition at Greenwich. Montague warned us that when the Commission met on 26 July we were likely to go into a category of project that would be placed in a pool that would get the go-ahead only when matching funding was in place. Possibly we would go into a category, acceptable in principle, on which further work would have to be done before consideration in the next round. Our analysis was that, if an unequivocal commitment from the Commission could be secured over the following month or so that the project would be given the green light subject to matching funding, the effect would be electrifying and funds would start to flow.

The next visit was from Sir John Hall and Simon Jenkins for a little over an hour on 10 July. Our much shorter presentation on this occasion had to be curtailed even further for Sir John Hall, whose aeroplane arrived late. I had a hurried discussion with him as we scampered round the site before he speeded away to hear about the rugby ground. I found an opportunity later to talk to Simon Jenkins, who from the start was sympathetic and in the autumn confirmed in writing that he supported the Opera House.

8   Design and Development

The Commission continues to be attracted by your project and, once our requirements have been met, looks forward to working with you in partnership to achieve your objectives.

Jennifer Page, August 1995

At the beginning of the third week in July 1995 I wrote a long letter to Jennifer Page about the three main points that had emerged during the visits of the three Commissioners: Where was the funding to come from? Did the project enjoy broad support? And could it be built on time and to budget? Our funding strategy involved securing some £12 million of binding pledges by July 1996, with the balance of our £40 million target being secured over the following three years. I made it clear that our target for pledges would be critically dependent upon the Millennium Commission expressing unequivocal support for the project in principle at an early stage. Delay in our receiving that commitment to much beyond the end of September would put our timetable at severe risk. I made it clear that, if it was the policy of the Commission to limit its grants to 50 per cent of capital and to exclude any endowment element, we would be left with a gap of £15 million. I argued that, with the exception of the £5 million we were seeking to raise for WNO, all the Trust's funding could properly be defined as capital if the Trust was thought of as a business requiring an adequate capital base on which to do business.

We needed an endowment because we would not be receiving an economic rent for the large part of the building that would be occupied by WNO. We believed that the theatre itself could be run without subsidy and was capable of making a profit provided it was launched debt-free. I pressed the possibility of joint funding on the basis that if the Millennium Commission would not fund the endowment then it would be reasonable to seek Arts Council funding for the premises occupied by WNO. I confirmed that we had made an application for £5 million of European funds which would partially close the £15 million gap. I gave details of the widespread support that the project had generated; and of the remarkable community and education programme that was now taking shape, and finished with a commentary on the construction programme.

Just over a week later we received the first signal that all was not well. At the time we did not realize its full significance, but looking back, I think that it was then, at a meeting that she had with officials of the Arts Council of Wales on 1 August, that Jennifer Page revealed that the attitude of Commission officials was unhelpful and not based on any real understanding of what was involved in managing a project of this magnitude; or perhaps it was that she simply did not understand the difference between a large, well-resourced permanent organization that could go a long way forward on its own, and one that was dependent on there being a genuine partnership if the funds were to be raised and the problems overcome. After the meeting, one friend in the Arts Council organization described her as frosty and acerbic, scathing in her description of our bid, which she said was poor and gave no evidence that the development could be costed or any indication that it could be funded. We were, she apparently said, developing a scheme on spec!

Well, it was certainly true that we had to speculate as far as support from the Millennium Commission was concerned. Not only was Jennifer Page demanding that further work should be done on the design concept before the Commission would agree to a detailed appraisal review, but she expected that matching funding had to be in place before the Commission would commit itself. She did not believe that the Commission would allow its funds to be used for the endowment. About the only mildly positive remark that she made was that she did not rule out Commission support for the Opera House and the rugby ground. Despite the fact that she received a strong statement from Arts Council officials about the importance of the Opera House, she was later to assert that there was a lack of support for the project from the Arts Council of Wales. Emyr Jenkins told me at the time that the Arts Council was fully behind the project and that direct financial support was ruled out only because it was understood to be against the Commission's policy.

The Commission had met and decided on its next step on 26 July before that encounter in Cardiff. Jennifer Page's comments to the Arts Council may therefore have reflected what had been said by Commissioners. She wrote on 9 August to say that the Commission had expressed continuing interest in the project; but while encouraged by our progress to date, it had concerns about our state of readiness. It was not prepared to initiate a detailed appraisal but would give us until 12 February 1996 to prepare additional information, when the project would be considered alongside and in competition with applications received in the Commission's second round. We had to provide a design and cost estimates within a 5–10 per cent contingency, and a lot more detail and proof of funding. There had to be further commitments from our co-funders. It was some encouragement that the letter contained the sentence: 'The Commission continues to be attracted by your project and, once our requirements have been met, looks forward to working with you in partnership to achieve your objectives.' To us it seemed a pretty strange kind of partnership.

Adrian Ellis promptly went back to the Commission on our behalf. In a letter on 11 August he described our experience since the application as being rather disorientating. Communication with the Commission had been limited – that was a polite way of saying that we practically never heard from our case officer – and no authentic discussion of the enormous challenges that we were facing and how they might be overcome had been possible. This was because of the generalized and formulaic nature of all written communications and the hurried, partially informed and often contradictory nature of all oral exchanges. He pointed out that we would be ready with the required information by September; and spelled out the cost, logistical dislocation and uncertainty that would be caused by a delay into 1996, which would put the Trust in a dangerously exposed position. He repeated a point that I had made in my letter about the absurdity of the proposition that we should take the design to RIBA Stage D, which would have cost us about £2.5 million, and asked that the project should be assessed in early November. He made a number of positive proposals for dealing with the problem of the endowment, confirmed that we expected to know the outcome of our European funding in September or October, and re-emphasized the need for a reasonably firm level of commitment from the Commission if our fund-raising efforts were to be successful.

This sharp exchange had a positive outcome. The Commission agreed to review our application on receipt of more detailed costings of the design, with the probability of a decision before Christmas. As

I commented to the Trustees, that meant that the project would effectively be made or broken over the following ten weeks or so. I also told them that I thought it would be necessary to secure, in addition to the European grant, some £5–£8 million of private-sector funding before the project went back to the Commission.

We were not having a peaceful August. Geoffrey Inkin at this stage was positive and encouraging in his support, but the CBDC had its own funding problems, and I therefore wrote a strong appeal to William Hague at the Welsh Office. It was partly an appeal for money and partly an effort to brief the new Secretary of State. My letter described the scale of the crisis through which we had just passed. The Commission's original letter had seemed to be almost a knock-out blow for reasons that I set out:

> First, in order to reduce the risk to the Commission it would place on the Trust (and CBDC which is funding it) a very large additional burden without even the certainty of detailed appraisal, let alone approval; second, the magnification of risk was likely to mean that our private funding for the design phase we had just started would be withdrawn; third, against that degree of uncertainty we could not recruit the skilled fundraisers we urgently need if we are to raise the private sector funding that is required. The ability to raise this money is so crucially important that [that] seemed a particularly devastating blow; fourth, it is not practical or economic for a design team to start work on a large project only to stand down for a prolonged period while the future of the project is determined.

I made it clear that, even though it now seemed that we were on a better course, we still urgently needed the assurance that we would receive from the Welsh Office or from the CBDC the money needed to take us through to the end of the year. Following that exchange of letters, the money was forthcoming, and we went ahead with the design and other work required with all speed.

We also prepared to receive a visit from Virginia Bottomley and fellow commissioners on 31 August. We were now dealing with our third chairman of the Commission, and also our third Secretary of State for Wales. I told William Hague that we hoped to be able to persuade the Commission of the importance of the project (on which more than £1.5 million of Welsh Office money had already been spent) in terms of urban renewal and tourism, and to close a huge gap in Welsh cultural facilities.

As a result of a conversation between Peter Rogers and Doug Weston, the director of Millennium projects, that took place before the commissioners arrived, we received another signal that there were still basic differences of approach to be overcome. Weston still had to be persuaded on the issue of RIBA Stage D; and he seemed unaware that the arts and heritage lottery funding bodies were supporting quite large projects with pre-funding, a level of ignorance that was alarming. He also raised a new point when he said that, in addition to the Commissioners being concerned about our ability to raise funds, they were worried about the issue of élitism. He believed that the Opera House should be 'more for the people' and should be used by school choirs and miners from the Valleys! I did not know whether to laugh or cry over remarks that displayed such profound ignorance. Apart from the fact that the miners had virtually gone from the Valleys and that the great Welsh choirs made regular appearances at the St David's Hall, that comment suggested that our detailed explanations of the way in which the building was to be used had simply not been read. As for the nonsense about élitism, perhaps the best general rebuttal that I have seen in print on the topic had been written by one of his own commissioners, Simon Jenkins, in *The Spectator*.

The presentations to the Commission on 31 August followed the previous pattern except that the principal briefing session and lunch took place in the new NCM building with its magnificent views of the site and across the Bay. Virginia Bottomley was accompanied by Lord Glentoran, the Earl of Dalkeith, Patricia Scotland QC and Jennifer Page. As far as we could judge, it went very well, and Virginia Bottomley emerged to speak warmly of the project to the waiting TV cameras and the press, and to confirm that the Commission would judge the Opera House and the rugby ground separately on their merits. It was possible for Cardiff to have both. A week later we received confirmation that if the required information was submitted by 8 November, the appraisal and report to the Commissioners would be available for their meeting on 20 December.

On the day before the Commission visit, the client and design teams, twenty people in all, had packed into Zaha Hadid's small studio for a review of current ideas and to identify specific issues that needed to be addressed. It was not an ideal form of gathering, and we never repeated it in quite that form again, but it was certainly educational in the way it illustrated the complexity of what we were about. In addition to three trustees (David Davies, Alun Michael and me) and Mandy Wix, and our advisers Adrian Ellis and Peter Rogers, there was the architect and two of her assistants, two from Ove Arup Structures, one from Arup Acoustics, and two more from other parts of the Ove Arup organization, two from Theatre Projects Consultants, three from Tillyards (Hadid's quantity surveyors) and Alan Lansdell from Bovis. Alan Lansdell's appearance on the scene was particularly significant, because not only was he being paid for at risk by Bovis, but he came with tremendous references from George Christie at Glyndebourne. We sent the team away with encouraging words to get on with the job.

The numbers would have been even larger if the meeting had taken place later in the autumn, because by then the Percy Thomas Partnership had joined the design team at the invitation of Zaha Hadid and with the warm approval of the Trustees. They were to provide the large-scale resource that was needed to back up Hadid's own staff. In the light of subsequent events it is worth recording that the Trustees were informed that the basis of the arrangement was that both teams were to work hand in hand together, 'the only basis for a healthy long-term relationship'. The joint company that they formed was structured on a fifty-fifty basis with equal representation on the board of directors.

All sorts of other things were happening alongside, including joint liaison meetings with CBDC and endless discussions about the design of the Oval Basin in front of the Opera House and the termination of Bute Avenue (the new boulevard running from the city centre), and the need for the CBDC to take belated decisions about car parking in the area. These were matters which could have major impacts on aspects of the design.

Other work was being carried forward on community activities and education, on reviewing the market assessments and in preparation of the business plan, and all the time on the central overriding priority of fund-raising. Among local business people who were particularly helpful in this respect was Alfred Gooding, a brave and energetic south Wales industrialist. During the autumn we succeeded in recruiting Jane Harris, the very talented development director of the National Youth Orchestra, James O'Rourke from the Welsh youth organization, the Urdd, and Claire Feazey from inside

WNO. Jane Harris and James O'Rourke, who gave up their previous jobs, were gambling with their careers and taking great personal risks, and they did so because they believed that this was the most important arts project in Britain at the time. James O'Rourke brought with him the welcome contribution of the Welsh language and a deep involvement in Welsh cultural affairs. Among the Trustees Gwyneth Jones was a particularly enthusiastic fund-raiser, seeking out support from among her contacts around the world and proving an inspirational hostess at events. One notable occasion was built around a Pavarotti concert at Llangollen when, with the help of Lady Trevor and the late Lord Trevor, we entertained some potentially large givers at Brynkinalt, the Trevors' magnificent home near Chirk in north Wales, took them to the concert and introduced them to the singer after the event. On that night over 7,000 people were packed into the grounds of the International Eisteddfod, with another 3,000 in Singleton Park in Swansea watching and listening to the concert on television screens connected by a BT link. A year later there were similar crowds in Llangollen to hear the great Welsh singer Bryn Terfel. Why do people say that opera is élitist?

At our away day, held in the Albert Hall in September, we were able to involve all the Trustees in what was going on and in preparing for the future. It was here that we took the fateful decision not to change the name of the building, at least for the time being. Many other topics were discussed as well, including the appropriate form of management structure for the new theatre, and the way in which the responsibilities of the receiving house and WNO might be appropriately allocated. These were not simple issues, and they aroused strong feelings. When we were discussing matters of this kind it was a tremendous help having trustees like John Tooley and Patrick Deuchar with their immense experience. Experience, however, was not always a receipt for calm deliberation and easy agreement.

We had a long and vigorous debate on the question of what size the pit should be and how many players could be accommodated beneath the stage. With the need to house a full Wagnerian orchestra the question was important, affecting as it did the number of seats in the auditorium, the relationship of the conductor to the musicians, the balance of orchestral sound and the voices of the singers, and the distance of the singers from the seated audience. Carlo Rizzi and Anthony Freud had strong views which were broadly supported by

John Tooley. The architectural team and our theatre consultants were unhappy with what they proposed. I realized that there had to be a compromise, just as there had to be between an ideal acoustic for opera and the quite different acoustic needed for musicals. The second compromise was easily reached, and there was an acoustic range that could be achieved with moving panels on the walls. The first issue for a time caused me greater difficulty, until suddenly Dennis O'Neill interjected sharply, 'Don't take too much notice of the damned conductors; they don't care at all about the singers. We have to sing across the pit with all those musicians thundering away.' Like Boadicea, Gwyneth Jones swept down in support, diverted for a moment from her own particular hobbyhorse that all the walls should be made of wood. I suddenly realized that the musical experts were divided and that there was hope yet for the musically nearly illiterate chairman.

In mid-October I addressed a packed meeting of the Cardiff Business Club in the Grand Hotel in Cardiff. With an audience of several hundred, I took the opportunity to give a broad review of the project and to appeal for support. The editor of the *Western Mail* was present, and later in the week that newspaper printed the speech virtually in full across two pages of the newspaper. I said that the story of the Millennium bids for the Opera House and rugby ground illustrated our ability in Wales for disagreement and argument, and our self-destructive tendency to spend so much time suggesting a different course that we sometimes missed the main chance. Believing that it was possible to have both schemes, I expressed regret that one or two connected with the WRU were putting it around that it was necessary to campaign against the Opera House to achieve their ambitions. The Opera House was needed because there was a black hole, an extraordinary void, in the facilities for the people of Wales, who were uniquely deprived among the people of Britain, Europe and North America, of anywhere on their own home territory where they could see a large musical, let alone dance or opera, on an adequate stage. I found it difficult to understand how anyone with the power to influence events could want to deprive the people of Wales of a facility regarded as essential by almost every major city and certainly every capital city in the developed world.

How innocent I was! Russell Goodway, the Labour leader of the county council and prospective leader of the new unitary authority to replace it on 1 April 1996, was not present while the speech was delivered, but chose to enter during question time afterwards. He was hardly in his seat when he rose to say that he could see no need for the building, and that the Labour group, at a meeting that had just concluded, had decided to back the rugby ground. There was a great deal of support in the room when I suggested that perhaps it would be a good idea if he were to read what I had said before taking up that kind of position. Russell Goodway was a member of the CBDC as well as the county council and his intervention was an indication of the forces we were up against. Even the newly won support of the editor of the *Western Mail* did not quite compensate for such hostility in high places.

In one section of the speech I described the trail-blazing steps we were taking to involve local communities in the process of producing a great building in their midst. Our programme during the design and construction phases had the object of exciting an interest in the physical progress of the building and in what would take place within it. In the visitors' centre there were to be workshop stations fitted with the latest technology, so that youngsters could learn about the business of design and develop their own skills. There were to be school projects and teaching packs that could be used country-wide, drawing together those involved on the site, artists and members of the public, to create a sense of ownership from the word go. We had met with over fifty local groups to talk about their ambitions and hopes. We expected the rehearsal spaces, particularly the main production rehearsal room, to be used for events, including shows created by the community. We were bringing together in one building a world-class opera company and community activity reflecting a wide spectrum of content, style and ethnic mix.

I used the speech as an opportunity to present the principal changes to the design. In response to changes made by the CBDC to the road layout, the main entrance had been moved to face Bute Avenue to provide a striking entrance façade for those approaching from the city. The spaces for the access and participation activities, the restaurant, the cafeteria, and VIP and hospitality rooms had been moved to the side of the building facing the Oval Basin. There would be magnificent views from the restaurant on the third floor towards the sea and towards the dramatic glass front of the auditorium with its grand staircase and foyers. We had doubled the size of the cafeteria, which would now open into the concourse on the inside of the building and directly out into the Oval Basin square to provide a link with, and magnet for, local people and visitors to the inner harbour area. I described the new parking arrangements and floated the kite that we would like to find a better use than for car parking for the dramatically cantilevered wing confronting Pier Head Street.

I gave an account of the way that the auditorium was being developed for the expected audience of 78,000 people each year for opera and 345,000 for other entertainments. The great auditorium with its huge sheet of glass and views of the grand staircase and foyers inside would present a memorable shape to the world, illuminated and glowing at night, with the matching prows of its encircling wings complementing the similar prow of the NCM building. I concluded by saying that this was a once-for-all opportunity never to be repeated. The world would look on with astonishment if we threw away this chance by arguing among ourselves which was the better project. For us to lose both would be a particular absurdity. I refused to take part in a competition, a row or an argument. If others did that and we failed, our friends would despair and our many critics would simply laugh at us. Huge numbers of people wanted this building and the events that would happen within it. The next generation would want it. I asked for help at that crucial moment to make certain that we did not sell short the next generation.

One quaint convention of the Cardiff Business Club is that after the main address the unfortunate speaker is asked to speak again to those invited to stay on for the dinner that follows. I gave them a version of the drama by way of verse and a character well known to all Welshmen – Crawshay Bailey. The original Crawshay Bailey was an eighteenth-century Welsh ironmaster who stood for Parliament and provoked a scurrilous poem from his opponents. The poem did not prevent his election but it fathered a whole family of verse, some of it not suitable for mixed company, that has entertained those attending rugby club dinners and similar functions ever since. My additions to this genre seemed to go down well, and later stimulated the Welsh artist Kyffin Williams (who had just published a book of his own Crawshay Bailey inventions) to give me a picture of the characters involved.

Verses Delivered to a Dinner of the Cardiff Business Club

> Crawshay Bailey's sister Mabel
> Lived beside this tower of Babel.
> In London town the great Commission
> Impatiently refused permission.
>
> Crawshay Bailey's brother Vernon
> Criticized the rich Commission
> As they couldn't put it up
> Twickenham took the Welsh World Cup.
>
> Crawshay Bailey's numerous cousins
> Signed petitions by the dozens.
> Tasker Watkins wise and brave
> Commanded Wales, 'Unite and save.'
>
> Crawshay Bailey's Western Mail
> Loudly proclaimed we must not fail,
> While Crawshay Bailey's nephew Russell
> Made the county council bustle.
>
> Crawshay Bailey's Opera Trust
> Said both the projects are a must.
> They lent Bryn Terfel and scrummed together
> To win the score that will live for ever.
>
> Crawshay Bailey's people all
> Gathered in the great new hall
> Where opera chorus made a din
> To celebrate the World Cup win.

Kyffin Williams placed under his drawing an additional verse:

> Crawshay Bailey's brother Nick
> Said it really made him sick
> When Welsh Rugby had a grouse
> About the Cardiff Opera House!

In mid-October we were greatly encouraged to read the wholly positive assessment produced for the Commission by Richard Pulford, who had been appointed on the advice of the Arts Council of England. His central conclusion was that the project fully warranted support from national lottery funds. He also made the point that the fact that the application had to be considered by the Millennium Commission placed the Opera House proposal at a material disadvantage in comparison with those bidding for Arts Council lottery funds. We did not know at this stage that this comprehensive report and the equally favourable assessment independently produced by Roger Tomlinson, appointed on the recommendation of the Arts Council of Wales, would not be laid before the Commissioners. They would have to make do with a 'summary' prepared by Jennifer Page which remained confidential to the Commission, a situation that I regard as shocking and indefensible.

Meanwhile good progress was being made with the design. The costs of the arts centre were now on target, but the parking was proving expensive, so that at the end of October total construction costs were a little above our objective. On the other hand we were able to reduce the endowment on the basis of the reappraisal of the business plan. At the beginning of November we submitted a large quantity of supplementary material for the detailed appraisal. Most of the documents concerned the project-management arrangements, together with the development of the design and associated costs since the submission of the application in April. The market assessment and financial projections had been updated by the accountants, Grant Thornton. In addition we provided updated material on the Access and Participation programme, on fund-raising and on site acquisition, together with copies of the economic appraisal undertaken by KPMG in 1991 and the 'Next Steps' report undertaken by AEA in 1993.

We maintained our bid at £50 million, but it was now less heavily front-end-loaded because we had increased our bid for European funding to £12 million in response to encouragement from the Welsh Office to do so, and were confident that we would have £5 million of private funding committed by the year's end, a confidence that was to prove well justified. The private-sector fund-raising would cover the balance of the capital costs, and a prudent £7 million endowment would ensure that there would be no call on public funds for any operating deficit. The total cost of the project, including endowment, in first-quarter-1995 prices, was £81.73 million. The total capital cost was £75 million. We kept the WNO bridge fund of £5 million out of the bid. Of that sum £800,000 had already been raised.

At this stage, just to complicate matters (though just how badly we did not then realize), KPMG withdrew as assessors on grounds of conflict of interest less than a week before our first scheduled meeting, and BDO Stoy Haward were appointed by the Millennium Commission in their place. The documents we submitted covering the construction and costs were impressive, and reflected the strength of the design and the project and construction teams. Cost issues had been covered by a partnership that had been formed for the purpose by the firms Gardiner & Theobalds and Tillyards, both front-ranking specialists in their field. I wondered subsequently whether, if the Trustees, and particularly those who were bankers, had spent more time on the financial report, it would have been significantly different; but I very much doubt it. Anyone who has been involved in business will know the difficulty of preparing annual budgets and three-year plans for existing, well-established businesses, that stand up to the uncertainties of a changing economic environment. We were having to prepare a plan and make financial projections for a new business that would not start to operate in its new premises for five years, and those forecasts had to look a further three years or more ahead. I do not think that it would have been possible to produce a better business plan.

We were now entering the difficult final phase of detailed discussion with the Millennium Commission's staff and their assessors. Work continued on the design, and Alun Michael and Patrick Deuchar returned to their old job of inveigling good images out of Zaha Hadid. Much of the burden of the exchanges with the Commission fell on Adrian Ellis and Peter Rogers. I, with the help of Alun Michael and David Davies in particular, had the more enjoyable task of getting positive results out of the warm but lively partnership that had now developed between architect and client. It involved very frequent visits to Zaha Hadid's studio and much debate, usually conducted with the ever patient and capable Brian Ma Siy. Zaha Hadid would suddenly arrive in the middle of these debates, usually to introduce a new element of drama to our discussions.

The team was not having a smooth ride with BDO Stoy Haward, who had come in at short notice and had not had the time to read many of the papers, so that they did not appear well informed about the market in which we had to operate. Their attitude was rather well summed up by the question put to Mandy Wix: 'How can you prove to me that people will want to come to such a run-down part of Cardiff?' I wonder if the same question was asked about the far more run-down Millennium Exhibition site at Greenwich. By this time, as they should have observed, a remarkable transformation was under way in the Bay area, and the description given was already ludicrously inappropriate.

I had also had a challenging discussion with Cameron Mackintosh, with whom I had been trying to arrange a meeting all the summer. He made a number of useful suggestions about the backstage arrangements, but was strongly critical of the interior of the auditorium. He wanted a house with 2,000 seats, all with good sight lines, preferably on no more than two levels, and with the audience brought well forward towards the stage. A house suitable for opera with its requirement for intimacy, a particular acoustic and limited overhangs, tended to produce an auditorium with high-level seating and a good many seats at the side of the building, which was far from ideal for musicals. We had addressed the acoustic require-ments, but clearly needed to do much more to produce seating arrangements that would satisfy Cameron Mackintosh. Within a structure whose external characteristics were now settled, there was still ample scope for most of the changes that would be needed within the auditorium. I sent the design team away with a brief to increase the seat numbers to 2,000 when the theatre was configured without a pit, to reduce seating at the highest levels and to modify the internal layout to meet the principal criticisms that had been made.

We received another alarm signal about attitudes within the Commission. Apparently Jennifer Page was again saying that the Arts Council of Wales were not fully behind the project. Richard Lloyd Jones and Emyr Jenkins confirmed the absurdity of the charge. Emyr Jenkins had by then held two meetings with Jennifer Page. It seemed that the idea had arisen because the Arts Council, which had been looking at the possibility of helping to fund aspects of the project directly related to WNO or to the use of Welsh craftsmen and materials, had abandoned the idea for the time being. They had done so because, when Jennifer Page was asked directly whether it was still the policy of the Commission that it should be the sole funder, she had replied in the affirmative. Next I heard that Simon Jenkins had been saying that we did not have an adequate professional team, and that not enough work had been done on design and costing. I hoped that if he had made such a comment, it was because his information was out of date, so I wrote giving him the facts. He replied that I must have been misinformed and that he remained most enthusiastic about the project. His sole concern was with the speed of progress.

In mid-November I decided that we had to challenge the Millennium policy on 50 per cent funding that had been so strongly criticized by the Arts Assessors, and which threatened to destroy us. The Commission, unlike the other lottery funding bodies, was limiting its grants to 50 per cent of capital costs; the others were going to at least 75 per cent. We had raised the issue on a number of occasions since the submission of our original application and had expressed our concern directly to Virginia Bottomley during her visit to Cardiff. I now wrote to her and to Michael Heseltine. I told them that it would be most unfortunate if the project were to fail simply because it was in Wales and not in England. I told them of a conversation with Grey Gowrie, the chairman of the Arts Council of England and a former Minister for the Arts, who had suggested that if there were overriding reasons for limiting the Millennium grant to 50 per cent, there should be early discussions with the Arts Councils of England and Wales to find a solution. I said that even those in Wales who were not ardent supporters of the application would be dismayed if it failed because it was in Cardiff, when an application to the Arts Council of England for an identical amount in Bristol might succeed.

To Michael Heseltine I sent a separate letter saying that he would understand the political sensitivities (in the widest sense). I argued that the case for amending the Commission's rule on 50 per cent funding was exceptionally strong and provided the simplest solution. I received a letter in response from Virginia Bottomley saying that the Commission had considered my representations and decided that it was not prepared to admit exceptions to the rule in the first or second rounds of competitive bidding; and that it was unlikely to modify its policy in the planned third or any subsequent round. I was shocked by such a gross failure of judgement, almost incredible from two such senior and experienced political figures, and hardly less so from the other commissioners involved.

I spoke at once to Virginia Bottomley and then wrote a strong letter of protest. I expressed my dismay that I had apparently failed to get over to her and to her colleagues the injustice of the combination of policies being pursued. I said that I could not believe that when the original policy decisions were taken it was realized that they would make it impossible for a large arts project to be funded in Wales, Scotland or Northern Ireland when lottery funding for similar projects was available in England, or that this could be one consequence of the separation of the English and Welsh Arts Councils. Virginia Bottomley had written about the grief that would arise from any attempt to unpick the existing rules. I responded that there was abundant grief in a package of policies that disqualified Cardiff from having a project that could have been adequately funded in Bristol. We were not seeking some variation of the rules that would place us in a position of advantage over other projects; we were simply asking to be granted the same upper limits as would be the case in England. If there were reasons for not raising the Millennium limit, all that was required was an agreement that the Arts Councils, from their share of the lottery, could fund the balance above 50 per cent.

I said that I would not be alone in considering it an indefensible situation if this immensely important project was killed simply because of a rigid application of an initial set of policy decisions whose consequences had not been adequately thought through. I finished the letter by saying that I could not disguise my sense of disbelief and indignation that the government was apparently prepared to contemplate not just the loss of one of the outstanding Millennium projects yet presented, but a political disaster in Wales as well. Surely it was the task of ministers to ensure that absurdities and injustices of that kind did not occur, and if there was a will I was certain that a solution could be found. It was not; and these ministers were, less than a month later, to rub salt in the wound that they had inflicted, by saying that the reason they rejected the project was that they did not believe that we could raise all the money needed.

The Secretary of State for Wales received a copy of my letter but, if he did anything about it, the fact was not made known to us. It was also remarkable that with the notable exception of Alun Michael, not one Labour Member of Parliament raised his voice in protest. In Parliament the only Welsh Member who joined Alun Michael in the battle for the Opera House was Dafydd Wigley, the Plaid Cymru member for Caernarfon in north Wales.

There was a meeting with Jennifer Page at the beginning of December when she identified the uncertainties that still concerned her. During that discussion it emerged that the Commission was now thinking in terms of a headline figure of around £94 million. The difference between that and our figure of £75 million was accounted for by the fact that their figure was at out-turn and not current prices, and included a contingency of 10 per cent rather than our figure of 7.5 per cent. Our contingency provision had been reduced to 7.5 per cent on the advice of our professional advisers because of the stage in the design development that had been reached. The principal concern, however, focused on the income and expenditure projections after the opening of the project. Jennifer Page and Bob Stubbs of BDO Stoy Haward seemed to have discounted the knowledge of the immensely experienced Arts Assessors, our own Trustees, the WNO and our advisers. They also set on one side the discussions that we had held with potential suppliers of musicals, and instead produced a range of projections all based on worst-case assumptions. In a five-page letter, plus annexes, to Bob Stubbs on 14 December, Adrian Ellis dealt point by point with these and all the many other points that BDO Stoy Haward had raised in their search for absolute certainty in business projections that looked into the first decade of the next century.

All this was worrying, but we thought that the ground had been well covered and adequate reassurance given, particularly because of our acceptance of a formula that had come from Bob Stubbs himself. We said that we were quite prepared to accept partnership funding from the Millennium Commission limited at this stage to an amount that would take the project to the completion of the design phase prior to going out to contract, conditional on an adequate portion of the private-sector funding being in place by January 1997. We estimated that it would cost £5.5 million to complete the design stage. We would raise £2.75 million ourselves and draw down £2.75 million of Millennium funds. With the design work completed and tenders in, two uncertainties would have been removed: the costs would be known within narrow limits, and our fund-raising capacity would also be known. We were asking the Commission to risk no more than £2.75 million, not much more than had already been risked by the project's backers.

While these financial issues were being thrashed out and BDO Stoy Haward taken through the business plan, there was great activity in the Hadid studio in London. During November and December work was under way on a new model, and we got down to examining materials and discussing finishes. We became more and more confident and excited about the stunning impact of the design. The new model was completed just before the Commission met to decide our fate.

1. *Zaha Hadid's perspex model: the initial design (by permission of the Office of Zaha Hadid)*

2. *The final Hadid model (by permission of the Office of Zaha Hadid)*

3. *The proposed Museum wing (by permission of the Office of Zaha Hadid)*

4. *The Norman Foster model (by permission of HTV)*

5. The model of Manfredi Nicoletti's design (by permission of HTV)

6. The model of Itsuko Hasegawa's design (by permission of HTV)

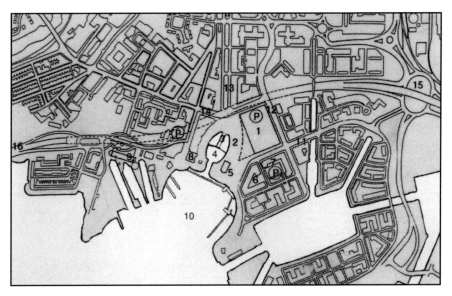

7. Ground-plan of Cardiff Bay (from the Cardiff Bay Opera House Architectural Competition archive)

Key

1 Opera House site	9 Techniquest
2 Oval Basin Piazza	10 Inner Harbour
3 LRT Terminus	11 Pierhead Street
4 Oval Basin	12 East Bute Street
5 Pierhead Building	13 Bute Avenue
6 Hotel	14 James Street
7 WHCSA Building	15 PDR Roundabout
8 WIMM	16 PDR

Parking Ⓟ

9   *The Design*

Jewels in a crystal necklace – and a living room for the city.
Zaha Hadid

The final days of waiting before the Millennium Commission's decision were an opportune moment to look at the design into which so much effort had gone, and on which so much depended. The arguments which had been so fierce had raged around a competition scheme and crude early models. We now could show people the model of a building that was true to the original concept, but which had been refined and developed by the creative partnership of architect and client. The long process of perfecting the design was not yet complete, most significantly within the auditorium itself, and the New Year would produce a new proposal for the South Wing; but we had reached the point at which we had a design and model ready for judgement.

The opera houses around the world that I have visited make an impact in three quite separate ways: visually from outside; in terms of the drama they create as you move through foyers and upstairs towards the auditorium; and in the theatricality of the auditorium that helps create the mood for the performance that is to follow. The best of them are exciting and memorable in all three respects; if they also provide comfort, outstanding acoustics and good sight lines, they provide the ideal setting in which to enjoy the performances of great artists. Because they tend to be large buildings, the older ones opulent in design, and because they frequently have rather grand entrances, very few of them appear inviting to the casual passer-by. Almost all of them are entirely secretive about the artistic activity taking place inside them; the only clue that opera houses are busy performance factories, in which a multitude go about their different tasks, is provided by the sight of musicians entering by small back doors, or large lorries loading scenery in bays behind the building. In Cardiff we told the entrants to the competition that we wanted a building that was not only outstanding in the first three respects, but one that would invite people in by night and day to be the hub and driving engine of activity in the Bay area. The brilliance of Zaha Hadid's design lay in the fact that she succeeded so well in meeting these requirements and in doing something that was not specified, which was to let the world see and be excited by the activities of the resident company and other visiting companies as they prepared to perform.

Zaha Hadid, with her preoccupation with city design, placed her building firmly in the context of the street-block master plan prepared for the CBDC, giving it a definite edge that formed an absolutely appropriate boundary to the Oval Basin Piazza, but broke down the hard barriers that usually separate a building and isolate it from the world and people outside. Access and views under and through the curtain wall were to lead into the heart of the site. This opening of the perimeter wall would have been most dramatic where the building faced the Oval Basin, the Pierhead Building and Cardiff Bay. Here the ground would have sloped gently up through the opening from the public space around the Oval Basin and into the central courtyard, with its mixture of hard material and soft landscaping around the auditorium and the principal rehearsal building. This opening in the perimeter would have provided intensely dramatic views into the great sheet of glass, the grand staircase, and foyers of the auditorium, with its soaring prow, and out from those foyers to the sea beyond. On the roof of the main rehearsal space in the courtyard was to be an area for outside performances; projecting above were the 'jewels' in what Zaha Hadid described as a 'crystal necklace', revealing in a unique way the fact that this was a building alive with practice and performance. Below this courtyard, which became known within the Trust as the bubble, there was to be a large concourse, again not hidden, but open and welcoming through a great curve of glass around the main entrance and through other glass doors and the cafeteria from the Oval Basin. The foundation of the architectural concept was formed by two principles. The first was the idea that the building created its own context by using a glazed perimeter wall which was then raised and opened out to draw the public into the curved landscaped courtyard. This is what Zaha Hadid described as a 'living room' for the city. Not only was it to be an extension of the civic spaces and public squares of Cardiff, but also the roof and shelter for the spacious concourse underneath, fully enclosed and protected from the elements. The intention was that the public should come into this concourse not just to see the performances, but also for exhibitions, recitals, to attend a dance class or a schools programme, or just simply to have coffee and enjoy the views out into Cardiff Bay. The second principle was that the building should open up the activities inside the opera house which are normally hidden. For instance, the performance spaces such as the production rehearsal facilities, the orchestral rehearsal rooms and the main auditorium, were to be articulated as sculptured forms, set into the glazed perimeter wall 'like jewels in a necklace'. '

The main entrance and drop-off point for visitors was moved after the competition to the elevation facing directly on to Bute Avenue, the formal link back to the city centre; this was a logical consequence of decisions taken at that time by the planners about the manner in which Bute Avenue would terminate at its Bay end. As a consequence, the Opera House was designed fully to confront the mile-long avenue, and visitors' first view of the building as they approached from this direction would have been of the sweep of the entrance and, above it, two large production rehearsal studios revealing glimpses of performers at work and theatrical lighting, an indication of the excitement of the performance to take place within. The view down Pierhead Street would have been of the remarkable cantilevered southern wing projecting out towards the Pierhead Building and the large mural on the building's rear wall. The many visitors approaching on foot from around the Bay would first have seen the auditorium, with its great glass wall, framed by the cantilevered wings on each side, dramatic in impact and magnetic in the manner in which it would draw them in to explore the complex and the events happening inside.

The original models unfortunately gave no accurate impression of the materials that would be used or of the effect that they would have. The architecture of the building was based upon the simple contrast between the transparency of the glass and the sculptural volumes of 'fairface' concrete. Great care has been taken in researching a method of achieving the fine, smooth finish of this concrete which is easy to use and cost-effective. It is a surface that ages gracefully, without the weather staining that occurs with ordinary concrete. Probably the best-known recent building using the material is the headquarters of MI5 at the southern end of Vauxhall

Bridge in London. As clients, we were impressed by the remarkable way in which it is possible to vary the texture and colour of the material to precise limits. The same kind of attention was paid by the design team to the glass façade. It was the intention to use a natural-coloured glass with good thermal values and low solar gain for the wings, the glazed areas of the concourse, and the auditorium. The south-west façade of the wing facing the Oval Basin was to have special glass to shade the spaces from solar glare and help reduce thermal gain. Whereas the overall forms were to be in fairface concrete, some special items were to have a deliberately different treatment. For instance the undersides of the jewels were to be in vivid colours; the elevation of East Bute Street was to have a mural in mosaic executed by Welsh craftsmen; and the courtyard was to have a rich tapestry of materials including Welsh slate. The approaches to the building would also have made striking use of contrasting patterns of colour and material.

Within the building there was to be generous provision for cloakrooms, lavatories, shops and restaurants, and ample foyer space with well-positioned bars. The audience would enter the auditorium directly out of the concourse or up the grand staircase with its magnificent views of the Bay. The first two requirements of a great lyric theatre, an exciting exterior, and interior arrangements that are both dramatic and practical, were therefore amply met. The auditorium was another principal feature that was going to be dramatic in its impact. The proposed space was large, larger than Covent Garden, about the same volume as the Coliseum (the home of English National Opera), comparable to La Scala, but a good deal smaller than the Opéra de la Bastille, all of which have more seats. The asymmetrical layout, though helping to create interest and sense of tension in the seated audience, was the subject of much debate and analysis by the Trustees. I went to look at asymmetrical theatres in America. We concluded that gross asymmetry, particularly in the stalls seating, created significant difficulties, but that some asymmetry added to the architectural interest and could be combined with a seating pattern that met our objectives. At the competition stage we left it to those entering to decide whether a traditional horseshoe shape or the more unusual fan shape provided the best solution. The new Glyndebourne is a good example of the horseshoe, and illustrates both its advantages and its problems:

particularly suitable for the operas of Mozart, it is wonderfully intimate, creating an atmosphere among the audience of shared experience and achieving exactly the right relationship between performers and audience. However, there is a price to be paid: a good deal of the stage is not visible to those seated on the outer flanks of the semicircle, and some of the seats nearest to the stage have such limited sight lines that they are restricted to use by house staff.

The fan shape is better suited to large Wagnerian performances and for the modern musical. It tends to be less intimate; but it is easier to provide the majority of the seats with excellent sight lines. The theatre consultant has two principal objectives in the design of an auditorium: intimacy and sight lines. These objectives are often in conflict; and are also influenced by the acoustic requirements of opera, which preclude large overhanging galleries. In a modern opera house there is the added problem that it is desirable that the audience should be able to see a surtitle screen, although some American opera houses are now installing individual screens in seat backs. In many opera houses some of the cheaper seats are in upper tiers at a considerable height above the stage; but the producers of musicals like to have their audiences four-square in front of the proscenium. Zaha Hadid's auditorium combined some features of both the horseshoe and the fan, and its large volume left the designers with a good deal of room for adjustment and experiment. At the time of the Millennium rejection the original layout had been modified and much improved by the introduction of a sweeping stalls circle that reduced the number of stalls seats. Further work was being undertaken on the positioning and layout of the overhanging boxes, and in December 1995 I had asked for the total number of seats to be increased to 2,000, and for the upper galleries to be modified to make the theatre more suitable for musicals. All this was part of the normal process of developing a design in partnership with a client and making the compromises that are an essential part of any good theatre design. Working not only with a particularly creative architectural team, but with the immensely experienced Ove Arup Acoustics and with Theatre Projects Consultants, I am certain that this would have been an outstanding auditorium, to be compared with the very best in the world.

There were to be three alternative pit sizes, and three elevators to provide the various pit configurations: a small orchestra pit with twelve to eighteen musicians in the open, a normal pit allowing about sixty musicians in the open and an extra-large one with about ninety musicians in the open. In each case additional musicians could be accommodated under the stage. The acoustic of the auditorium was to be capable of adjustment for different types of performance by means of movable panels on the back and side walls, which would also have provided a striking visual element. The first and most influential need for a good acoustic is appropriate room volume to achieve the reverberations required, but the change in the comfort requirement for seats in a modern building has added to the volume, and this is why a new opera house will tend to have fewer seats than an earlier building of comparable size. The design to be used in Cardiff would have helped to counter the damaging impact on the acoustic of deep overhangs by using open holes at the back of the tiers to help in feeding reverberant sound under the balconies; these holes would also have allowed the variable absorption panels to be lowered down the full height of the rear wall without obstruction. Not only the auditorium, but also the rehearsal rooms, studios, orchestra pit, stage and fly tower, the technical rooms and front-of-house areas were all planned with great care to achieve acceptable acoustic standards.

The stage, with a structural proscenium opening 18 metres wide and 10.5 metres high was designed to function for a major opera company performing in repertoire, for major musicals with heavy scenic requirements, for ballet companies who need a ballet floor, and for a range of other activities. The effective working proscenium width would have been adjustable between 11 metres and 14 metres, and the stage would have had a clear depth of 18 metres. Provision was made for single-purchase counterweight flying; and, because the object was to be consistent with typical UK theatre requirements and most world-wide touring productions, it was not the intention to provide mechanized equipment in or under the stage floor such as revolves, elevators and wagon stages. The planning of the back-of-house areas produced efficient, practical spaces for both WNO and any visiting company. There was easy access from the loading dock, where up to three pantechnicons could park at any one time under cover, to the stage, to the principal rehearsal and production studios, and by elevator to the other rehearsal rooms and WNO production areas. The WNO accommodation in the wing facing Bute Avenue was provided with excellent access to the stage and fly-tower areas and to canteen accommodation shared with visiting companies.

A key element of the architectural design was the importance attached to drawing in and welcoming the public to the building. During the design-development phase the Access and Participation community programmes were moved into the wing facing the Oval Basin and the public open space around it. This meant that the public would have had access not only to the ground and auditorium areas but also to the raised wing with the most dramatic views overlooking the Oval Basin and Cardiff Bay beyond. They also would have had easy access to the principal rehearsal spaces, so that these could be used by outside organizations when not required by WNO. To supplement the Access and Participation activities, the public restaurant was placed on the top floor of the wing, with the large cafeteria, spilling out into the Oval Basin Piazza, below it at ground-floor level. The restaurant would have had magnificent views, in towards the glass wall of the auditorium, the grand staircase and foyers as well as out towards the sea. Seen from the ground outside, this projecting wing would have been an echo of the full-height glass elevation of the main auditorium, and thus there would have been two visibly active well-lit elevations revealing people inside using the building and its restaurants. This would have been recognizably a building supporting a wide range of public activities as a complement to the performing events. Immense trouble was taken by the design team to provide full access for disabled people to all parts of the building.

In the period of development following the competition, the parking was moved into the wing beside Pierhead Street. This was a radical move because the car park was now in a very prominent position in a 130-metre-long structure cantilevered out towards the Pierhead Building, and set off by four-storey-high steel trusses with infill panels of subtle horizontal louvres of steel. The layers of fine steel members would have created a vivid contrast with the glass façades of the remaining wings. The move made possible the replacement of the angled exterior ramp of the original design by internal spiral ramps. The arrangement fitted in well with traffic movement in the area; but it was an expensive form of parking, and I was not alone in thinking that there must be a better use for a part of the building that provided superb views across the Bay.

Much later in the story we were to find an appropriate solution which would have involved turning the wing into new galleries, a restaurant and an IMAX cinema for the National Museum, and siting the car park on Museum land a few hundred metres away. The two glass elevations of the Opera House would thus have been matched by a third with its own 'jewel' containing a Celtic boat recovered from the mud of the Severn estuary; and like the others, it would have revealed activity, light and colour to the outside world. Surely those three great luminous prows (and the not dissimilar prow shape of the NCM building close by) would have become striking, beautiful and easily recognized symbols of Cardiff around the world.

Zaha Hadid had taken great pains to ensure that her design suited the urban context in which it was sited. There can have been very few other buildings in which there has been more painstaking analysis of its purpose and of the internal functional requirements, or greater dexterity in providing for them. Her deconstructionist approach almost by definition implies a concentration on internal purpose, and it is only when that has been fully thought through and provided for that the components are put together to form a complete structure. A very remarkable feature of the events in Cardiff was the way in which the original concept stood up to the pressures placed upon it. As we sought to find the compromises that are necessary if different forms of activity are to take place within a single arts centre, and as we changed the brief to meet the special needs of WNO and the Access and Participation programme, the original component parts were simply moved around the necklace and the whole building became more compact and efficient. This, above all, was a building which would have worked wonderfully well as a great music theatre, a home for Welsh National Opera, a place in which a wide variety of community activities would have taken place, and perhaps above all as a 'living room' for the people of Cardiff and the hundreds of thousands of visitors whom it would have attracted each year from around the world.

10 *Rejection*

Those who carry out great public schemes must be proof against the most fatiguing delays, the most mortifying disappointments, the most striking insults and worst of all, the presumptuous judgements of the ignorant upon their designs.

Edmund Burke

The Millennium Commission was to meet on 20 December to decide our fate. In the week before, the final signals had been mixed. It was encouraging that we had been invited to the press conference scheduled for Friday 22 December and asked to send display boards and other material. Virginia Bottomley had indicated to at least one MP that we could expect good news, but there had been a telephone call from Michael Montague with the message that things were moving against us. We could only wait. There was no more to be done. The wait was longer than we had expected. We heard nothing on the 20th, and the next morning passed without news.

Tension mounted as the day wore on and we were still without news. I returned after lunch to my London office and checked the whereabouts of colleagues. Alun Michael was on the motorway to Cardiff. Adrian Ellis had set out on the longer journey to his cottage in north Wales in the company of his wife and baby daughter. The atmosphere in the Cardiff office was almost unbearable. Shortly after four o'clock Michael Heseltine came on the telephone to hold what he ominously described as an 'old colleagues' conversation'. Perhaps, when the memoirs come to be written we will discover whether Virginia Bottomley's nerve had simply failed at the prospect of speaking to me, whether Michael Heseltine had gallantly volunteered to shelter his colleague, or whether they simply drew lots. 'The Commissioners are a hard-nosed bunch', began my former colleague. 'I have got some bad news, but some good news as well. The bad news is that I am afraid they won't approve your project as it now stands: it all comes down to scale and uncertainty about the money; but the good news is that there is enthusiasm for the idea of an opera house and for what it will do for Cardiff. The trouble is that there is no enthusiasm for a project of this size and cost.' The Deputy Prime Minister seemed to be attempting to distance himself from responsibility for these hard-nosed ideas. I felt physically sick. It was no comfort to be told that the Commissioners were sympathetic to the idea of an opera house when they appeared to have mortally wounded a project that was the result of ten years of planning and research, and the skill and experience of a hugely talented team. I said that I was totally shocked and very angry.

He urged me to look again and try a new approach. He said that the new concert hall in Manchester which was now almost complete had cost only a little more than £40 million. I said that I knew it and had been to Manchester and discussed it with the local-authority team responsible for it. Did he really think that you could build an opera house with stage and equipment for the same price as a concert hall? Did he not know that our building included accommodation and rehearsal facilities for WNO, accommodation and performing spaces for local community activities and car parking? He was comparing the construction cost of a building almost complete by the end of 1995 with the estimated cost, including an allowance for inflation, of a building that would not be complete until the year 2000. He was comparing that building cost with the total cost of the Cardiff project, including endowment, start-up expenses and the WNO bridge fund. If this was the basis for the decisions that had been taken I was entitled to be angry.

He persisted, and appeared to show an astonishing lack of understanding of the nature of the project and what is involved in the development of a design from an original brief and concept to the final design and tender stage. Again and again he pressed me to come back with a much smaller and cheaper scheme. Again and again I pointed out that the brief to the architect was the outcome of prolonged research into what was required if the business plan was to be viable and we were to provide what was needed. I explained that you could not just chop bits off the design, which had already been drastically pruned to bring it within budget. We had had an international competition, and all the commended designs had been of the same general order of magnitude. The Millennium Commission had known from the start the likely cost of the project and the scale of the grant required, and if they were never prepared to consider it they should have said so before so much public and private money and effort had been expended for no purpose. It was impossible for the Trust to start again. We had spent over £2 million to get to this stage. To begin a complete redesign would be vastly expensive and we had not got the money. If the problem was that he and his colleagues doubted our ability to raise the matching funding, then I had to remind him that £20 million of the funding requirement was accounted for by his Commission's refusal to follow the practice of the other lottery funding bodies and give 75 per cent grants. Despite that, our very experienced and successful team of fund-raisers were confident of the outcome.

After nearly half an hour of repetitive discussion, it was suggested that I should speak to Simon Jenkins if I wanted another view. In private conversations over previous months Simon Jenkins had always indicated support, and had confirmed that support in writing. His attitude had been very similar to that of Michael Montague, another commissioner with whom I had been in contact. After my conversation I was not much the wiser as to what had led them to abandon their previous position and surrender to a majority view that seemed to have emerged only at the last moment. Jenkins talked vaguely about the weight of opinion, the scale of the project, and fund-raising. He mentioned unresolved design issues. I asked him if the Commissioners had been influenced by any personal hostility to the design; he said that the issue had not been discussed, but that it might have been in some people's minds. The Commissioners had seen the new and impressive model, completed only days before, on their way to the decisive meeting. Virginia Bottomley also confirmed that the design had not been debated and was not the reason for the conclusion that had been reached. My first conversation with her was brief, as she had to leave for an engagement, but she kindly telephoned me late that evening after a visit to the theatre, although not much more emerged on that occasion from a somewhat emotional and heated conversation.

While the earlier exchanges with commissioners were taking place, a letter had arrived from Jennifer Page setting out the verdict in more detail.

> The Commission notes that the outturn capital costs of the project are now agreed as being in the region of £94.86m, allowing for contingencies and for the capitalisation of the pre-opening costs. The Commission is not convinced that at this level of cost the project represents value for money for the investment of funds from the National Lottery.

It was typical of the somewhat slipshod approach of Commission officials that the figure was not in fact agreed and was £3m more than our own estimate. It subsequently emerged that the Commission had been guilty of some double counting.

The letter continued:

> The Commission also notes that, in the opinion of its advisers, the business plan fails to address a number of significant commercial issues and the design of the internal layout of the building is not yet fixed, with outstanding planning issues and the potential for significant changes to major elements of the building. The Commission noted your suggestion that a contribution of £2.75m on a risk basis towards the £5.5m cost of working throughout 1996 could allow these uncertainties to be resolved and to establish whether the necessary co-funding can be achieved from private and European sources. Thereafter, the problems of revenue support would remain to be tackled.
>
> After extended discussion the Commissioners unanimously decided that, on the grounds of value for money and the technical, business and financial uncertainties, they were not prepared to offer grant to this project. This is a great disappointment to the Commission which has indicated that it believed that a major lyric theatre in Cardiff was, in principle, capable of support with Millennium Commission funding, and which has devoted time and money to evaluating the proposals over the last few months; the Commission regrets that the case presented does not allow an offer of grant to be made.

There followed some words of sympathy and the offer of an urgent meeting to discuss the matter. It was odd that with that time and money spent in evaluating the proposals over a period of months the Commission had not previously found it possible to identify this long list of alleged shortcomings so that they might have been dealt with before the submission was finalized. In reality the Commissioners' advisers had indicated that they were broadly satisfied and, unlike the other lottery distributors, the Commission had never apparently seen it as their role to work with an applicant to bring a project to fruition. Looking back, it is hard to grasp the fact that the scheme submitted in April 1995 remained constant throughout the assessment process with the same fund-raising plans, the same design concept, the same theatre programme; but with revenue projections that actually improved. If anything, the scheme had been enhanced by the development of the Access and Participation programme and the probable addition of European money. In the New Year we were to take up the offer of an urgent meeting, and my account of that meeting provides the appropriate place to comment on this list of assertions, half-truths and distortions that was used to justify the Commission's own failure to grasp an opportunity to celebrate the Millennium with a great achievement.

In the mean time I had the unenviable task of breaking the awful news to Zaha Hadid and my colleagues. It was a good thing that Aileen Oates, my secretary, was still in the office and knew exactly how I would be feeling. A bottle of whisky arrived as if by magic, and my glass was kept charged over the next hour. Zaha Hadid, shocked though she was, reacted with astonishing courage and dignity. Her summing up of the situation the next morning was particularly apposite; 'It is a bummer. Why have a Millennium Commission at all? Do they want nothing but mediocrity?' Meanwhile Adrian Ellis had recovered sufficiently from the first shock and emotion to pull into a lay-by from which, over the car telephone, he gave good advice about our next moves and what we should say; but it was my wife, Ann, who played the key role in what happened next. When the invitation to attend the Commission's press conference had been received some days earlier we had decided that I would attend in London and that Alun Michael and other trustees would hold a separate conference in Cardiff. Later Commission officials produced the false story that I had gatecrashed their press conference. That was untrue; the invitation we had received to send representatives had no conditions attached, and when, on the afternoon before it was to be held, the bad news was finally and belatedly broken to us no suggestion was made that the invitation was withdrawn. My first reaction, born of shock and disappointment, was that I could not face it and that I would travel to Cardiff and join Alun Michael and the others there. Ann would have none of it: when I telephoned her at our Welsh home she told me very firmly and with her usual good judgement in a crisis that my place was in London; that was where the principal correspondents and commentators would be, and if I wanted national and international coverage that was where I must be. How right she was!

We not only dominated television, radio and press coverage in the United Kingdom that day and the next, but we hit the front page of the *New York Times* as well. The team worked overnight to achieve that result. Adrian Ellis, having completed the journey to north Wales and coped with the job of getting wife, baby and luggage into their holiday cottage, worked into the small hours before faxing commentaries and draft press statements to me and to his London office. By eight next morning his equally indefatigable staff were well on the way to completing the job of having everything ready for issue. Soon after half past nine I was in Great Smith Street with Jan Billington, Adrian's assistant, and Brian Ma Siy representing Zaha Hadid. Inside Church House we were greeted by the BBC arts correspondent demanding an interview. A room was found, and that interview, and another with HTV, went out almost in full for the lunchtime news bulletins and provided the material for other news reports later in the day. They were complete and in the can before Virginia Bottomley and Jennifer Page were in the building and excited correspondents drank their pre-conference coffee already aware that they had a good row to report.

Later, people told me that the interview was effective and that I appeared to be very angry; I *was* angry, and that in part was why the interview was effective. By now the Commission staff were uncomfortably aware that all was not well with a press conference that had not even begun. I found my old friend Robin Herbert, there as chairman of Kew Gardens, seated at the end of the front row, and I joined him to offer congratulations on his successful bid for the Kew Seed Bank. The press conference itself was quite brief, and there were only a handful of questions, though one from the representative of the *Western Mail* was sharp and to the point. The response from the Commission chairman was not convincing: 'On the advice of expert opinion we were not able to support it; there were too many imponderables. There were so many unanswered questions that it would not have been safe to put Millennium Commission money into the project at this stage. We cannot disregard the strength of professional opinion.'

I knew that the professional advice on construction issues was overwhelmingly favourable and that the two Arts Assessors had provided reports that were strongly positive; we had been left with the impression by the accountants who had prepared the financial appraisal that we had satisfied them on the major points. There appeared to be no more questions. Virginia Bottomley looked hopefully around the room and suggested that everyone disperse for individual interviews. I got to my feet and said that I would like to put one question: every camera in the room swung towards me. A Cabinet minister being challenged at her own press conference by an ex-Cabinet minister and former colleague was a sufficiently unusual event to be interesting. 'Why was the Commission not prepared to spend the £2.75 million over the next year which was all that we had asked for at this stage in order to eliminate the uncertainties that remained, and to make possible the construction of the only significant architectural project to have emerged so far from the Millennium process?' The response included something about having to accept the advice of professionals, but I had asked that question because the idea of removing uncertainty by funding through the design phase had come from the Commission's own professional financial assessor, the only one of their advisers that we believed might have produced a critical report.

As the press representatives gathered round me I gave vent to my deep sense of despair at the lack of vision, leadership and courage that today characterizes so many aspects of our national life. I said that we were angry. We had been told by the Commission that they were prepared to back a major project and that Wales would have such a project. We were now being told that the project was too big, although much bigger projects were being backed in London with risks that were at least as great. Furthermore no suggestion had previously been made that the project was too big and should be scaled down. We had been seriously misled by the Commission; there were no significant risks in this project that are not inherent in any large construction project of this scale and character; and by appointing a professional team of world class and huge experience we had minimized those risks.

By this time Heather Wilkinson, Jennifer Page's deputy, was hovering ominously. Her assistant had just told Jan Billington to leave because she was not welcome, something that she had not the nerve to say to me. Heather Wilkinson told one correspondent that the Commission feared that the project might become another British Library, a comment that was an unwarranted reflection on the design and construction team that was described on a later occasion by a representative of the Commission as the cream of the British professionals. Heather Wilkinson proved to be the most outspoken of those who sought to defend the Commission. She said that the Opera House Trust had been forecasting losses of several hundreds of thousands of pounds a year and, seemingly overlooking the fact that any operating loss was to be covered by an endowment, added, 'We are not in the business of funding white elephants; the project just does not work, nor would it have worked in England. There is not a problem with the design but the business case had large holes in it.' Later from more authoritative sources we were to have different explanations. At the time I felt that these were over-hasty responses on her part; but perhaps even that was an uncharitable judgement on someone who must have felt that she was having a bad dream. There can be few more shattering experiences for someone charged with organizing an important press conference for a government minister than to find that the conference is being dominated by a hostile critic whom you did not expect to find there. I confess that as we departed to hold further interviews outside the main conference room, Jan and I let our feelings go with a roar of celebratory laughter that eased our disappointment and anger.

Down in Cardiff Alun Michael and other colleagues were holding a conference for the local press. I took the train to join them at the meeting of Trustees which had been originally arranged in the expectation that we would be planning the next stage of the design process and fund-raising activities. I was surprised to be greeted with applause when I walked into the meeting soon after one o'clock. Apparently everyone had been cheered by the lunchtime BBC1 news, which had given full coverage of my angry outburst. We decided to take up Jennifer Page's offer of an urgent meeting, which was arranged for 28 December. With that we all departed for a gloomy Christmas holiday, during the course of which the telephone and fax never seemed to stop. The gloom of the Trustees was shared in full measure by WNO and Lucy Stout's fund-raisers, who had worked so hard and with such professional skill to raise the remarkable sum of £6 million in firm commitments without any commitment from the Millennium Commission.

Jennifer Page arrived at the Marriot Hotel in Cardiff on the 28th suffering from a nasty attack of flu, and with a team that included Bob Stubbs, a partner of BDO Stoy Haward, who had produced the financial appraisal, and Doug Weston, who had been in charge of our project for the Millennium Commission. Five trustees were present, Wynford Evans and Lewis Evans (with banking and business experience as substantial as that of any member of the Commission), Patrick Deuchar and David Davies (who at the Albert Hall and with the WNO had acquired a knowledge of the performing-arts business that was totally lacking among Commission members), Alun Michael and I (who could not be taught many lessons about the political, social and economic background); and we were backed up by Adrian Ellis, Anthony Freud, Peter Rogers, Geoff Thomas of Grant Thornton, our adviser on the business plan, and, of course, Mandy Wix, our indefatigable administrator. Grant Thornton's knowledge and experience of business plans is at least the equal of BDO Stoy Haward's.

Our sympathy with Jennifer Page, who was clearly ill, was genuine. She could have called the meeting off, but in the circumstances we felt that the production of some aspirin was an adequate expression of fellow feeling, and there was no need to pull our punches. We were told that the meeting had been arranged so that the Trust could be informed of the professional advice that had been given to the Commission, which had started out with the aspiration that it would be possible to build a lyric theatre in Cardiff and would have been genuinely happy to support the project.

Doug Weston on behalf of the Commission began by expressing confidence in the Trust's construction and design team, which he described as 'first-class, the cream of British professionals and construction managers, capable of managing and delivering the project within the agreed cost total'. So much for what Heather Wilkinson had said before Christmas about the Commission fearing another British Library-type disaster. He felt that there were a number of technical issues that were going to stretch the team, but these were marginal and none were insurmountable. There were no practical problems that could not be overcome or issues that could not be resolved. Weston made the curious remark that 'the building had been designed from the outside inwards' and not with functional space in mind, and this would create pressure. It was a remark that revealed a depressing level of knowledge about how our architect worked and about the way in which her designs are created. There can have been few buildings ever designed with a greater concentration on function and what happens inside. Zaha Hadid had broken down the structure into a number of separate functional spaces and put them together into her necklace of jewels. Working with her client, she had refined those structures and their relationships until we, our professional advisers and WNO were totally satisfied that they would work. Perhaps he did not mean what he said, but intended to refer to the unchallengeable fact that the necklace concept combined with asymmetry does create some wasted space, but our rigorous refinement of the design had already tightened it to the point where such waste was minimal. An even more extraordinary remark was that there should have been a detailed feasibility study; there had of course been several! It is a dispiriting experience to be rejected by those who do not appear to have looked at some of the most important parts of the very detailed submissions. While it was probably too much to expect that the Commissioners themselves would read all the documents, we felt aggrieved by our frequently repeated impression that their officials and advisers had not done so either.

Bob Stubbs of BDO Stoy Hayward criticized the lack of a fully comprehensive business plan, which he maintained should be based on a worst-case scenario. His own scenario appeared positively apocalyptic; against our projected annual deficit of £200,000, thought to be pessimistic by the Arts Assessors, and in any case to be covered by an endowment, he apparently estimated the loss as likely to be £1 million per annum, and suggested that £700,000 should then be added for an annual contribution to a sinking fund required to cover maintenance and depreciation. Of this, he said £1 million would be an immediate cash requirement, increasing at out-turn prices to £2 million per annum, requiring an endowment of between £7 million and £20 million. It seemed to the Trustees that one wild estimate was being piled upon another and absurdity added to absurdity. One thing is certain: no arts project in the country, and few if any arts institutions, could have survived an appraisal of this kind. One might have thought that the Millennium Commissioners would have smelt a rat, or at the very least recognized that some further examination was required of a judgement that contrasted so starkly with that of the very experienced Arts Assessors and all the other studies carried out by professional bodies over the previous decade.

That was not all. We were criticized for not having appointed a chief executive and a management team, which suggested that Mr Stubbs did not appreciate the realities of the situation that we faced.

He asserted that there had been no comparative analysis of similar theatre facilities in the United Kingdom. This was not the case: the analysis provided by the Comedia and Graham Morris reports had explicitly addressed the financial performance of a range of approximately analogous theatres. He said that we had not provided evidence to support the assumed divisions of risk and income between promoters and the Opera House managers. This had been the subject of detailed explanation which had been supported by our consultants, by theatre managers and by representatives of Welsh National Opera, which as a major touring company had every reason to be well informed on the subject. Mr Stubbs had previously very fairly admitted his limited knowledge of this particular subject: during the time when Trust representatives were attempting to remedy this he had asked Ms Judi Richards, then general manager of the New Theatre, Cardiff, to explain 'in not more than five minutes' the nature of theatrical contractual arrangements and of the deals done between theatre managers and visiting companies. She had done so after first asking whether she could expect him to explain his business as an accountant in not more than five minutes! Later, when we asked N. M. Rothschild to review our business plan and to identify any serious shortcomings in it, they said that the document seemed well prepared, with nothing obviously missing, but that the persuasiveness of the business case depended fundamentally on the market/revenue analysis, a subject on which Rothschilds do not have expertise or credibility. There is nothing discreditable about a firm of bankers or accountants admitting that there are subjects on which they do not have expertise or credibility. BDO Stoy Hayward is a firm of distinction; but they had been called in at short notice and not given adequate time to read or assimilate the very large quantity of material that we had provided. Even so, it does seem surprising that on these particular topics their judgements were so far apart from a formidable body of expert opinion.

The Commission should have paid more attention to the views of their Arts Assessors. We were appalled to discover that their reports were not apparently seen by the Commissioners. Richard Pulford, selected on the advice of the Arts Council of England, advised that the

project fully warrants support . . . there is good reason to suppose that the project as a whole is financially and operationally viable . . . ticket and product demand are likely to be sufficient to sustain the operation of the Opera House as a venue for opera, dance, musicals and pantomime . . . there are good reasons for supposing that the Opera House could break even financially.

Roger Tomlinson, selected on the advice of the Arts Council of Wales, agreed. He reported that it was

reasonable to project a near break-even out-turn for the operation of the Opera House . . . there is every reason to believe that the Opera House will operate within the parameters of most other major theatres in the UK, between a modest profit and a modest loss. Indeed there is reason to suggest the former with some optimism, rather than the latter.

Subsequently he confirmed in an article in the *Western Mail* that the Trust had 'presented a Business Plan which as an arts operation was viable'. We pressed Jennifer Page as to why these reports had apparently been ignored, and received the feeble response that both Assessors had strayed outside their own brief. The Commissioners only received a précis of the reports; I still wonder whether their true content was suppressed.

While the Arts Assessors had apparently been given a brief for their work, we were astonished to be told by Jennifer Page that the Commission had set its reporting accountants no criteria on which to base their advice. Mr Stubbs told us that, because the project lacked an underwriter, they were looking for the kind of business plan that a commercial firm would submit to a merchant bank if it was seeking risk finance in the markets, a plan that must be based on the ability of the Trust to finance from its own resources a worst-case scenario. Our two bankers, Wynford Evans (who later became chairman of the Bank of Wales) and Lewis Evans, joined with those with extensive experience of arts administration in criticizing this approach as completely unreasonable. It seems extremely unlikely that any other arts applicant for lottery funds was asked to jump such an impossible hurdle. David Davies commented that, with the criteria suggested, WNO could not have survived in any of the fifty years of its existence.

The New Year had started as badly as the old one had ended. While before, we had been shocked and bewildered by the

Commission's rejection of the scheme, we were now deeply angered by the inadequacy of the reasons given and by the confirmation of the fact that some of the most vital evidence – that from the Arts Assessors – had not been put to the Commission in its original form.

11   A Decision without Merit

*For backing or laying against a horse, for starting a new sporting club or a
new music hall, the money would have been found in a few hours.*

Col. J. H. Mapleson, after failing to raise the final £10,000 to complete his National
Opera House on the Scotland Yard site in Westminster (begun in 1875; outside
walls, which had been completed, demolished in 1888)

From a source close to the Commission we gained the impression
that there was serious concern within the Little Smith Street office
that we might take the rejection to judicial review on the grounds
that it was a capricious decision, as opposed to a judgemental
decision based on all the facts. In this case it seemed clear to us that
all the facts had not been given to the Commissioners. Our own
advisers also had very much in mind the question whether the
Millennium Commission was acting in accordance with the true
requirements of public service by encouraging an application at a
very large cost in time, effort and resources, much of it voluntary and
at risk, only to reject it without giving any form of reasoned
decision. The letter which the Trust received undoubtedly sought to
give away as little as possible about the Commission's reasoning, and
had probably been drafted with at least one eye on the possibility of
judicial review. We did, indeed, take legal advice about this
possibility, but decided that there was little to be gained. A judicial
review would only have looked at the fairness of the procedures and
not the merits of the decision, and even if there had been a
judgement in our favour, it would no doubt have been possible to
find new and more plausible reasons for rejection. However, for the
time being we kept the possibility in mind. Our immediate
conclusion on leaving the meeting with officials in Cardiff was that
the Commission's reservations concerning the design, planning,
construction and capital costs of the building all appeared minor,
and indeed it had been confirmed that they were all quite
manageable by a team that had been described as the 'cream of the
construction industry'. We were left with the impression that many
of the doubts concerning the post-opening financial projections were

caused by the analysis provided by BDO Stoy Hayward, which was in conflict with that provided by our own advisers and by the only two Commission advisers whose reports we had seen. We also believed that, through no fault of their own, the accountants had not had time to assimilate the material that we had submitted, and that undue weight had been given to their conclusions.

In a letter to Virginia Bottomley sent on 11 January 1996 I made these points clear and said that we believed that the stated grounds for rejection were wholly inadequate, and that if there were wider policy considerations which had not been articulated at the meeting we should be told what they were. We gave her a point-by-point commentary on the issues that had been raised in Cardiff. This ground has already been covered and the arguments need not be repeated, but my paper was praised by colleagues as a *tour de force*. If the Commissioners took the trouble to read it, they would have been fully aware of all the key points in our case. Unfortunately we were soon to gain the impression that a number of the Commissioners did not read it. I took the opportunity to remind them that

> The Trustees are not a casual group of inexperienced amateurs but men and women distinguished in our respective fields whose relevant experience in business, the arts and politics makes us well qualified to form judgements about the issues now being debated. We have provided ourselves with professional advisers for every aspect of the project who are among the very best available in Britain today. We have immersed ourselves deeply in the project and considered the options and the risks over a period of several years. As Trustees, we have even stronger motives than the Commission for making the right judgements because we have fiduciary responsibilities and many of us are likely to be involved in managing the building and ensuring that it is a success in the years after the Commission has ceased to exist. While we fully accept that the Commission must make up its own mind, we believe that the Commission's knowledge of this project and the experience of its members and professional advisers cannot be greater than our own. We therefore do think that our representations deserve the closest possible consideration.

I expressed the sense of grievance that we felt because we had been misled. The Trust had devoted much time and effort on the basis that the Commission had studied its original application and saw nothing in principle that would lead to a rejection – in other words the scale of the project was not at issue. The Trustees had taken note of the government's statement that it was intended that the Commission should back a number of great projects and that at least one of those projects would be in Wales. The Prime Minister had indicated that the Cardiff Bay Opera House Trust was an ideal candidate for Millennium funding. Although the Commission had backed a number of interesting projects, there had been a strange reluctance to back major new architectural schemes to celebrate the millennium. I concluded the paper with the statement that the overwhelming weight of professional opinion was in our favour and that there were no problems that were not capable of resolution. I urged the Commission to reconsider its decision.

As a result of this paper and a personal appeal to Michael Heseltine that he should meet me, the Commission agreed to meet us in their offices just before their regular January meeting. It proved to be a wholly unsatisfactory occasion: only a few of the Commissioners were present; Simon Jenkins was a particularly noticeable absentee; Michael Heseltine, when he finally arrived after dealing with a political problem at No. 10, was at his most imperious. If he had read the papers he was certainly not going to deal with the points raised. Virginia Bottomley did not give the impression of being in charge; Michael Montague no longer seemed the supporter he had once claimed to be. Perhaps Jennifer Page had realized that the advice provided by BDO Stoy Hayward was not solid ground on which to stand, and so the defence was based almost entirely on the scale of the project and our ability to raise the money, ignoring the fact that the scale had not altered since the application had been made almost a year earlier. Michael Heseltine reverted to his absurd comparison with the new concert hall in Manchester, apparently forgetting that we were building a lyric theatre, car parking and a home for WNO, and ignoring the fact that the Manchester hall was completed five years before we planned to finish ours.

I found it hard to keep my temper. Finally, when Michael Heseltine, after being pressed to confirm the real reason for rejection, again said that it was doubts about our ability to raise the money, I rather sharply reminded him that £20 million of the funding gap had been created by his decision to give us only a 50 per cent grant, although in England from the Arts Council we could, and almost certainly would, have received 75 per cent. It was rather like doubling the height of Beechers Brook and then questioning whether the horses will be able to jump it without risk. Virginia Bottomley's summing up was inconclusive, although she was emphatic that the Commissioners' personal views about Zaha Hadid's design did not influence their decision. She declared that she personally found it exciting. We interpreted her words as meaning that if we could prove our ability to raise the funds all was not lost. We also now did have agreement that the Arts Council of Wales could be brought in and go to 75 per cent for its part of the project if it wished. I therefore wrote her a brief letter informing her that we intended to rise to the challenge; but we still needed formal confirmation from the Commission that they would consider another bid if the project was to remain alive.

Colin Ford, the director of the great institution that had been recently renamed the National Museums and Galleries of Wales, had by then come forward with the basis of an idea that we believed would enable us to make a fresh approach to the Commission. He had suggested that new maritime museum galleries might be placed within the Opera House building, replacing the car park. Some initial discussions had taken place with the Commission. At the end of January Ann and I left for a holiday in Ethiopia. On the way to the airport I telephoned Jennifer Page and said that we had been considering challenging the Commission's decision in the courts, but that we wanted to avoid that and come forward with a revision of the scheme that might be jointly funded with other lottery funding bodies. If the museum project was included, the National Heritage Memorial Fund as well as the Arts Council of Wales could join the Millennium Commission. Would she confirm that an approach on this basis would be properly considered by the Commission? She was friendly in her response and gave me a positive reply, saying that it could indeed be considered in the next round. On the strength of that I telephoned Mandy Wix from London Airport and told her to press on with a study of possible options while I was away.

12 The Museum Proposal

Therefore let our alliance be combin'd
Our best friends made, and our best means stretch'd out.
William Shakespeare, *Julius Caesar*

When I returned from holiday it seemed that a phoenix might just possibly be rising from the ashes. The proposals made on behalf of the National Museums and Galleries of Wales by Colin Ford, their director, seemed to have real promise. A new Waterfront Museum to replace the obsolete Welsh Industrial and Maritime Museum had been an aim of the museum authorities since 1993, and a number of schemes, including the construction of a large IMAX cinema and waterside aquaria, had been discussed with the CBDC, which was simultaneously receiving alternative proposals from other organizations. The complexity of these discussions, the problem of raising finance for so ambitious a project, and a judgement that it would be unwise to bid for Millennium funds simultaneously with a bid from the Opera House Trust, caused the Museum Council to postpone a bid until a later round. Colin Ford's idea was that it might be possible to place some of the museum galleries and the IMAX cinema in the Opera House building. He was aware that the Trustees were keen to find a way of removing the car park from the Opera House and to discover a better and more attractive use for the south wing. The museum had land which could be used for car parking, and the idea of incorporating museum galleries within a centre for the performing arts was attractive. The scheme also offered the possibility of joint funding for the combined project from the Millennium Commission for the lyric theatre, from the National Heritage Memorial Fund (through the Heritage Lottery Fund) for the museum component, and from the Arts Council of Wales for the WNO accommodation. We now had an undertaking from Jennifer Page of the Millennium Commission that they would be prepared to consider a fresh proposal involving joint funding.

A year earlier the Museum, in an internal report, had identified the advantages to be obtained in combining the efforts of the Opera

House Trust and the Museum on their sites facing each other across the Oval Basin. These advantages included the large impact of a cultural quarter at the heart of Cardiff Bay, which it was thought would become a major British landmark development for the beginning of the twenty-first century. There would be the benefit of having a day-and-night attraction of broad scope, covering a wide spectrum from the performing arts to the natural sciences (which would take in the social and maritime heritage of Wales). This would be attractive for a wide audience. A co-operative approach to fund-raising would be more likely to be productive than one in which the two bodies were competing for the same moneys, particularly as it was thought that this broader project would receive wider support than had emerged for the Opera House on its own.

To put the Museum and the Opera House in the same building would provide even greater benefits. Both would be able to reduce their capital costs and overheads by sharing facilities, and there would be great opportunities for audience development for both organizations. The contribution that such a combined project would make to achieving the objectives for which the Cardiff Bay Development Corporation had been set up was so obvious and so substantial that one might have expected the idea to be seized upon with enthusiasm, and the backing of the Corporation to be immediately forthcoming for the development of these ideas and the work needed to bring them to a successful conclusion. Unfortunately the Corporation seemed only to have a single-minded obsession – to ensure that no building by Zaha Hadid was constructed in the Bay.

Zaha Hadid continued to show the breadth of vision that we had come to expect of her, and that her critics seemed incapable of matching. After three meetings at the end of January and early in February with museum officials, she wrote to me enthusiastically about that vision. She described how the range of activities now to be embraced in the building would impact on the design and the business viability of the project. She set out equally clearly what was required of the Trust in terms of a brief and organization if the necessary work was to be completed in the time-scale required. At the same time she produced her first outline plans and sketches, which in a thrilling fashion both realized the concept that Colin Ford had in mind and replaced the unsatisfactory car-park wing with an intensely dramatic and soaring prow of glass and steel. From this projected a characteristic Hadid 'jewel', splendidly displaying to the audience inside and out the Celtic Magor Pill boat recovered from the mud of the Severn Estuary.

An extract from a paper prepared by Colin Ford describing the planned use of the exhibition space gives a vivid impression of the drama of the design:

> The rest of the second floor is the climax of the visit – a stunning expanse of floor and glass, with extensive vistas over the Docks, the Bay and the City – and up to the hills and the valleys. Stepping into this space, it is soon clear that visitors are on the deck of an ocean-going ship (perhaps a liner from Cardiff's brief period as an emigration port, perhaps a coal tramp, perhaps a mixture of both, complete with funnels, deck chairs, lifeboats and exhibits from the maritime collections). On the north face is the top of the 'diamond' housing the Magor Pill boat. To reach it and its associated displays, one walks on glass: upon this can be seen exhibits (natural and man-made) discovered under the sea. Despite the drama, and the spectacle of the view, which will be a major selling point, this is a real museum with real artefacts. The prow of the ship is occupied by the ship's restaurant. Here, everything – decor, furniture, posters, menus, staff uniforms – interprets maritime history. Looking out over the Oval Basin, the oldest part of the docks, one sees historic boats or their facsimiles, and reads about them at one's table. The most spectacularly sited – and most informative – restaurant in Britain.

Zaha Hadid had emphasized in her letter to me that there was no intention to 'shoehorn the museum into the existing form of the wing'. Instead she would be designing a wing to suit very specifically the programme and function of the museum. Even at this early stage of the redesign the architect was responding imaginatively and creatively to the requirements and ideas of the client, just as she had already done with the Trust. During the previous period of our working together, she had created not just a very practical building and magnificent auditorium, but also in the facing wing another dramatically sited restaurant for the lyric theatre audiences, together with those other 'jewels', theatrically revealing to those outside the building the activities going on inside.

It all seemed very promising, but Alun Michael strongly advised that if we were to succeed with this revised venture we must try and obtain a wide measure of support from the local authorities and other representative bodies in Cardiff. He thought that the time might be right to put the past behind us. The Welsh Rugby Union had been successful in its Millennium application and the supporters of a new rugby stadium on the Arms Park site should no longer feel that the Opera House was a competitive threat. The mood of the press, too, had changed and the *Western Mail* had moved from the position of hostile critic to that of enthusiastic supporter. Inside local government there also appeared to be a fresh atmosphere developing. It seemed clear that we must accept Alun Michael's advice and take full advantage of his links with colleagues in the Labour Party. The Institute of Welsh Affairs had just produced a useful report on the extraordinary injustice of the policy of the Millennium Commission that limited its grant to 50 per cent of capital costs, and the Institute was anxious to help. It was therefore decided that a meeting of all the interested parties would be arranged by the Institute, with its chairman, Geraint Talfan Davies (the director of BBC Wales), taking the lead in making the arrangements. In the mean time Alun Michael encouraged Zaha Hadid to produce drawings to illustrate the exciting new proposals, while he simultaneously worked on a paper for the meeting setting out the options before us, and tried to persuade his political colleagues to come to the proposed meeting with open minds. The prospects seemed much more encouraging; but into this new environment of hope and expectation a bomb was about to be thrown.

13 The Ides of March

There now began an episode that was even more shocking than the Millennium Commission's rejection of the original scheme. The meeting organized by the Institute of Welsh Affairs was to take place on the afternoon of Friday 8 March. It was to be attended by representatives of the National Museums and Galleries, the Opera House Trust, the Cardiff Bay Development Corporation, the new unitary authority in Cardiff, just created by the reform of local government, Associated British Ports and its subsidiary Grosvenor Waterside, the Cardiff Bay Business Forum, Welsh National Opera, the Arts Council of Wales, the Wales Tourist Board, the Welsh Development Agency and the Cardiff Chamber of Commerce. At lunchtime on 6 March I took a call from Aileen, my secretary, in the office of the AA at Basingstoke, where I was attending a meeting of the committee, in the course of which she told me that Geoffrey Inkin, chairman of the Cardiff Bay Development Corporation wanted a meeting with me as soon as possible. She had explained to him that as I had a dinner of the National Rivers Authority in Bristol that evening and a board meeting there the following morning I would not be available in London on the Thursday and could not see him in Wales before the evening; she had therefore fixed a meeting with him for midday on Friday. It is surprising, in view of the importance of what, it later transpired, he had to tell me, that he did not speak to me on the telephone either on the Wednesday or the Thursday, or suggest that we met in Wales as soon as I could get there from my Bristol meeting. Instead he went off to London, where he asked Sir Keith Stuart, chairman of ABP, to join him for lunch. Over coffee he said that uncertainty about the project could not continue, and that he was therefore considering sending a letter setting out the views of the CBDC. He handed Sir Keith a letter which contained words stating that the conclusions had been agreed by the Corporation and the landowner. Sir Keith said that nothing in the letter had been agreed by the landowner, and that if the letter was sent to the Trust the words must be removed. Nothing was said about the letter being sent to others. He did not contact Alun Michael, the deputy chairman of the Trust and the local MP, who was in London that day, or Wynford Evans, the other deputy chairman, who was in Cardiff. This was not the usual way in which Geoffrey Inkin conducted business: ever since, as Secretary of State, I had first given him the opportunity to use his talents in public organizations in Wales, he had made a practice of telephoning me frequently to discuss problems and seek advice. It was not to be so on this occasion: instead we met in Cardiff soon after midday on Friday 8 March, only four hours before the scheduled meeting at the National Museum at which the future of the project was to be discussed. It was a day appropriately close to the Ides of March.

Geoffrey Inkin's words to me at our meeting came as a bombshell; those words broadly duplicated the contents of a letter, which he handed to me as he spoke, that presented a most pessimistic account of the chances of success if we attempted to go forward with the Hadid scheme, concluding that 'the chances of success of the existing proposals are extremely limited', and that therefore another and totally different approach was required. The analysis was incomplete, and controversial as Inkin had not checked the facts with the Trust or ascertained whether there was other information that might be available to it. He had attended the first, but not the second, Trust meeting held in February. It was a conclusion reached without any discussion with the chairman or any member of the Trust that he and his Corporation had set up and financed up to that moment with substantial public funds. Worse was to come: Inkin then handed me a letter that he told me had been circulated that morning to 'all the principals' of the organizations due to be represented at the afternoon meeting. That letter contained the words: 'We have concluded on the grounds of its high total cost, its apparent lack of support by the new unitary authority and the public and the absence of backing from the Millennium Commission, that the Hadid scheme should be set aside.'

Inkin appeared to have pre-empted the discussion planned for later that afternoon, prejudged the response of the Commission and of the other lottery funders and the public to a revised scheme that they had not yet considered, and which the CBDC had not examined in detail or discussed with the Trust, and precluded the possibility of any rational and balanced consideration of the options that day or at any other time. The decision which he and his board seemed to have taken (at its March meeting) was likely to involve the writing off of over £2 million of public money and considerable private funds invested by Bovis, ABP and others, without consultation with the Trust. Most of that money had been directed specifically to the competition and the development of the Hadid design. Furiously angry, I immediately walked out of his office and made a number of telephone calls, first and most urgently to Alun Michael who had played a key role in setting up the Institute meeting and had been devoting enormous effort to regenerating the project and local authority support for it. Astonishingly we then discovered that he had not been judged a principal and had not been sent a copy of the letter. He was as angry and appalled as I was.

I had arranged to meet my wife and some friends at the National Museum in mid-afternoon so that we could visit an exhibition of pictures by the Welsh artist and poet David Jones before I went upstairs to the Council room for a meeting now doomed to fail. Ann found me still shaking with shock and anger. I handed her the letters, and after reading them she turned to our friends and said, 'Now Nick has been stabbed in the back by some of his oldest friends.' It was true, but there were others equally badly wounded, and none more so than poor Zaha Hadid.

Not long afterwards, in a letter to a friend, I summed up my views about the conduct of those involved in this unsavoury act. I wrote of a decision that I and others

> find inexplicable, inexcusable and a grave error of judgement, not least because of the failure properly to consider all the options that might have provided protection for the large sum of public money that has been invested in the project . . . I remain unable to understand how the CBDC could possibly believe it right to take a decision of such importance without any discussion with, or warning to the Trust which they had set up and financed; or why the Corporation should think it sensible to pre-empt discussion at the Institute meeting and kill the project in advance of that meeting. To hand me a letter four hours before the meeting and not inform Alun Michael at all was just an added offensive twist to the tactic adopted.

The meeting that followed was even more disastrous than I feared it might be, and was described later by one of those present as about the worst that he had ever experienced in a long public career. Alun Michael had prepared a characteristically comprehensive and competent paper setting out the history of the project, describing the work of the Trust in carrying through the brief prepared in 1991 by Geoffrey Inkin's committee, and analysing all possible options. The paper made it absolutely clear that the Trust representatives would come to the meeting with completely open minds, hoping that the revised Hadid scheme incorporating the Museum wing would be considered on its merits. Many of those attending the meeting had not yet seen the new proposals, so recently prepared, or heard a detailed explanation of revisions that not only changed the design in a very fundamental way, but also transformed the nature of the bid and the proposed funding arrangements. The meeting had appeared to provide an ideal opportunity to present these changes and explain them.

Alun Michael's paper contained a careful analysis of the financial, legal and practical consequences of taking a number of possible courses. We had envisaged that it would be circulated by the Institute of Welsh Affairs to all those attending several days before the meeting. In the event Geraint Talfan Davies, the chairman, decided not to distribute the paper in advance on the grounds that even so balanced a presentation might lead to allegations in some quarters that the ground was being unfairly prepared in a way that would prejudice a genuinely open debate. However, Alun Michael did send direct to Anthony Freud of WNO, Colin Ford of the National Museum, and the county council three drawings showing the present state of the revised Hadid design incorporating the Museum galleries and Imax theatre. The CBDC was fully aware of what was going on. What was proposed had been discussed at the first February Trust meeting which Inkin had attended, and on the previous Sunday I had told Hugh Hudson-Davies about Alun Michael's paper and of our determination to approach the Friday debate with open minds. Hugh Hudson-Davies was a member of a small working group set up by the Corporation to consider the future of the project.

That the meeting followed a disastrous course was not the fault of Geraint Talfan Davies, who was in the chair and opened the meeting with the statement that the Institute had always wanted a centre for the performing arts and that he assumed that everyone present could agree with that general objective. Gareth Jones, also representing the Institute, had hardly begun to elaborate on the proposition when he was challenged by Russell Goodway, the 36-year-old leader of the new unitary authority and one of the local-authority members of the CBDC. 'How do you know that there is a need?' he asked, adding that he had seen no convincing evidence and still needed to be persuaded. Alun Michael spoke of the detailed studies and reports since the early eighties that provided a wealth of evidence; Colin Ford, director of the Museum, referred to the examples of Bradford, Manchester and other cities; David Davies spoke of the evidence gathered by the Inkin committee; Alfred Gooding, a leading Welsh industrialist, spoke of the wider interest beyond Cardiff. But Russell Goodway remained obdurate. It was made abundantly clear that, whatever might be the pro-arts policies of Labour authorities in almost every other major city in Britain, this particular local-authority leader appeared to have other objectives. We had got away to a bad start, but it was decided that the Institute would prepare a paper setting out the available evidence.

Geraint Talfan Davies then reported the contents of the Inkin letter, which a majority of those present had not seen, and which David Davies and Anthony Freud of WNO had only seen shortly before the meeting began, and asked for the reaction of the Trust. Alun Michael outlined the contents of his paper, clearly describing all the realistic options and the problems that had to be faced. He pointed out that we had very little time, and asked if any of the alternatives to the Hadid scheme could possibly be achieved in the time available. Any prospect of success was dependent on our acting together: if we could achieve total unity then we might succeed; we must stop behaving 'like ferrets in a sack'! Roger Thomas, representing the Museum, said that his council were the supporters of something that was going to happen; he did not think it possible to get a consensus around Hadid; the CBDC had put a nail into that possibility! Alun Michael challenged that argument and again asked that people should discuss the options without prejudging Hadid. That prompted Inkin into an attempted explanation of the CBDC's actions. There had been, he said, a small group considering the problem since January, and it was pure coincidence that the process had come into focus in parallel with arrangements for this meeting; not completely in parallel, he might have added, since the process was structured so as to make it certain that a conclusion would be reached in advance of the meeting, without any proper consultation with the Trust or adequate consideration of the new proposals. He did not, needless to say, add anything of the kind, but instead denied a suggestion that there had been a conspiracy, and produced the surprising argument that the letter that he had circulated that morning to principals had been written in confidence. He agreed with an analysis that I had given of the likely costs and practical difficulties that would have to be faced if a fresh start was made, but said that there were other options. He appeared to be thinking in terms of a commercial lyric theatre, although he referred to the possibility of Arts Council and private participation.

Russell Goodway then made his second intervention of the meeting. The significance of the local authority in this connection, he said, would be as a sign that the project had strong public support, but for his authority to give its backing, any applicant would first have to prove that it had the public overwhelmingly behind it. In other words we were faced with a situation in which we had a local authority which under its present leader was not going to provide the leadership to create public opinion, but was only going to follow on behind if the public demanded that it should. One person present spoke of the contrast of the approach outlined by Russell Goodway with that of Salford, where the council's leadership of public opinion and its financial support had been the foundation of the successful Millennium bid for the Lowry Centre. Newcomers to this whole affair, such as David Rowe-Beddoe who was present as chairman of the Welsh Development Agency, were learning very quickly about the obstacles that we had faced so far.

At this point David Davies very quietly reminded us of WNO's central interest. This provoked another intervention from Russell Goodway. He saw no reason to support WNO, which could look after itself as far as he was concerned. Later, as the debate continued about how a fresh project might be initiated and a client group created, Goodway said that he did not believe that WNO should be involved, and added that no one should look for a local-authority contribution to either capital or revenue.

It was clear to everyone by this time that there was no possibility at all of gathering support behind Hadid, and that the prospects of a successor body to the Trust being able to achieve anything worthwhile in the tight time-scales required for lottery funding were extremely bleak. It seemed clear to me that the project was dead, and that the only sensible course now was to go away and let the air clear. As Richard Lloyd Jones sagely observed, the debate would not die; he did not know if we could resolve the problem now, though people would think that we should be able to, but sooner or later the demand would re-emerge. Probably the only person present who could not recognize the demand and a compelling need at that time was the new leader of the local authority. Geraint Talfan Davies urged us all to avoid comment that would lead outsiders to say that Cardiff was a Clochemerle unable to cope with a large project. Alun Michael said that he agreed that we should do our best to avoid people commenting on that uncomfortable truth! By now Geoffrey Inkin had already left, ironically to host, as chairman of the Land Authority, a large party at that night's performance by WNO at the New Theatre. Michael Boyce, his chief executive, talked on about putting a client group together. I left, also to go to the New Theatre, and to tell the press representatives waiting on the steps of the museum outside that we had failed and that there was no common ground among those at the meeting that offered any reasonable hope that anything worthwhile could be rescued from the wreckage.

In a statement I issued three days later I expressed my thanks and appreciation to the many people inside and outside Wales who had worked so long and so hard on this immensely worthwhile project, and who shared my dismay at what had happened. In particular I drew attention to the way in which our efforts transcended differences of political loyalty, and paid tribute to the representatives of the county council and the City of Cardiff who had played a full and constructive part. The late Alun Davies, representing the city, was a particularly tireless contributor to our efforts. It was also the moment to express my particular appreciation for the contribution of Alun Michael who, on behalf of his constituents and the community, could not have done more.

Once again I had the mournful job of bringing bad news to Zaha Hadid. A few days later she wrote a generous letter to the Trustees. After describing the situation as incomprehensible and expressing bitter disappointment, she went on to refer to the special working relationship that had developed between the design team and the

Trust: 'This rapport is the basis for creating great architecture and, in our case, has helped to drive the development of the competition scheme into a design that is tough, functional and unique.' She finished by saying: 'You have been a marvellous client and I want to thank you, above all, for having such great faith in our work.' That faith existed not because she won a competition, but because we discovered for ourselves by working with her the quality of her work and the fundamental soundness of the original concept. That was particularly true of Alun Michael, who began as a critic but became one of her strongest defenders. In my response to her letter I said:

> We, too, have greatly enjoyed working with you and have been grateful for the splendid and positive way in which you responded to the sometimes testing demands of the Trust. I believe that the relationship grew into a fruitful partnership and that it would have produced a very great building . . . I do not believe that many design concepts can have been subject to such severe examination, or have come through that examination so well.

I added a particularly heartfelt tribute for the contribution of Brian Ma Siy 'whose work was of the highest quality and who acted so admirably as the principal link between the client and the other professionals involved'.

A good many of those who criticized the design did so because of the judgement they formed of the original model, and out of ignorance of the way in which a design concept is developed and grows in quality through the partnership between a good architect and a strong client. There were others unable to broaden their minds to accept any architectural vision that differed from a tradition with which they felt familiar, and these curiously included some who respond positively to challenging forms of modern art and music. There were as well many, notably within the Development Corporation and among local politicians, who simply decided that they knew what they liked and that 'over their dead bodies would this building be built'. None of those critics were at the ICA in London that March to hear a brilliant lecture by Zaha Hadid in which she explained to a distinguished audience her creative ideas and the way in which the Opera House design, including its further development for the museum project, had evolved. My wife, who had not previously heard Zaha Hadid talk about her work or seen the recent work on the design, came away from it – and an examination of the latest models and drawings – thrilled and inspired. She was not alone. Among the general public not all minds were as closed as among its so-called leaders and representatives.

In the *Western Mail* on 14 March there appeared a letter from two ordinary lovers of opera and art that summed up the tragedy better than anything else that I have read. I do not know John and Daphne Pavitt, but they represent those who have been betrayed by those responsible for the destruction of the Hadid scheme. They wrote:

Last night we saw and heard the WNO's brilliant performance of *Cavalleria Rusticana* and *Pagliacci* at the New Theatre in Cardiff. At £10.40 for a seat in the gods – almost every one occupied by ordinary people – this was no élitist experience. During fifteen years we have enjoyed most WNO operas, The Northern Ballet Theatre, *Carmen Jones* and *Evita* from the same seats. As we left the theatre we thought of the opportunity of a real opera house or lyric theatre (call it what you will) in Cardiff Bay.

Are we to be disappointed? This morning your paper told us that 'a closed meeting' had decided that the design by Zaha Hadid should be abandoned, the Opera House Trust replaced, and a cut-price project launched if there were sufficient public backing.

At one blow, Cardiff will lose a building hailed as the only worthy architectural landmark for the millennium that has so far been seen; an established team that has worked unremittingly to promote, test, improve and commend the project; a fitting home for the most consistently successful cultural enterprise seen in Wales during the last half-century; and a theatre that could bring Bryn Terfel and other international artists back to Wales in the year 2000.

Why has Cardiff so cruelly rejected this great opportunity? We suggest that a self-appointed group of short-sighted businessmen set the trap; a mistaken rivalry with the Welsh Rugby Union sprang it; and a potentially philistine local authority (not yet in office) seeks to administer the death blow. You, Sir, have not helped by your late conversion from opposition.

Is it too late? We hope that the proposed final test of public opinion will, unlike the previous poll, ask fair questions, reach a fair sample of the people and lead to a fair conclusion. If it proves that Cardiff deserves to have this opera house, let our businessmen, councillors and journalists help to make it a reality. Then we will cheer them in the gods.
John and Daphne Pavitt.

14 The Press and Public Relations

The role of the press in reporting, and attempting to manipulate, public opinion cannot be ignored, and the recent tone of lamentation ill becomes those who helped to generate such largely negative opinion.

Jan Harris, *Planet*

I have a huge collection of press cuttings about the Cardiff Opera House. Confronted by these great piles of paper, my initial reaction was to run away from the task of compiling a coherent account of this aspect of the story and to limit myself to a few paragraphs about its impact on the final outcome. However, with the first draft of this book almost complete, I received from Bob Skinner a very comprehensive report that he had prepared on the subject. Bob Skinner, a public-relations practitioner with experience going back over forty years, was the Trust's public-relations officer from March 1995 until its demise a year later. His account is of particular interest because he was not involved in the events surrounding the setting up of the Trust and the architectural competition, but was in the thick of things when the Millennium Commission rejected our application. I am grateful for his permission to use his paper as the source material for this chapter, and to quote his opinions.

From the start the Trust realized the importance of public relations, and during the course of its first year it appointed Hill and Nolton, a London public relations consultancy, which drew up a detailed programme and a strategy to be followed. Before the competition was concluded, Hill and Nolton was replaced by Stratton and Reekie in London, and Quadrant, who also acted for the CBDC, in Cardiff. Early in 1995 financial pressures and a belief that Quadrant was finding it increasingly difficult to act for both the Trust and the CBDC led to the appointment of Bob Skinner on a part-time basis. From that time on public relations were handled in-house by Bob Skinner and Mandy Wix. The Trust's Public Relations Committee was chaired by Alun Michael, who devoted much time and effort to the handling of the local press, with which, as a former journalist and a very active politician, he had close contacts. Invaluable help was also given by Sue Harris and Patrick Deuchar.

Among the key objectives identified by the first consultants was 'to position the building of the Opera House as inevitable', to be achieved by developing active support among businesses, local, regional and national government, educational institutions and the local community. It was a carefully thought-out, comprehensive strategy that was accepted by the Trust, but its implementation was handicapped by a lack of resources. Despite the appointment of consultants and the considerable amount of time and effort devoted by Alun Michael and his colleagues, there was never the opportunity to mount a sustained public-relations campaign; and later, when opposition emerged in the shape of the Welsh Rugby Union's National Stadium, the Trust found itself facing a barrage of criticism, often fuelled by misleading information and crude simplification or distortion of the issues involved.

Press coverage of the developing story from start to finish was extensive. Much of it was serious and well informed, and there were a large number of articles about Zaha Hadid, the design and the Trust's handling of events in the more serious national newspapers. In general, the arts and architectural correspondents were in favour of both the winning design and the whole concept of an international opera house in a distinctive world-class building in Wales. Several writers hailed the Hadid design as the only one worthy of being accepted as one of the twelve United Kingdom landmark projects sought by the Millennium Commission. There was an even more extensive and much more heated series of articles and much correspondence in architectural and building journals. Well informed though some of the articles were, they probably had little impact on events, though on balance they probably strengthened the position of Zaha Hadid and the Trust. One national tabloid took a wholly hostile line. The *Sun* viewed with disdain the aspirations of élitist opera fans, ignored completely the ambitions of those in Wales who wanted to enjoy musical theatre, and maintained a strident campaign to ensure that the 'people's' lottery cash did not go to providing exclusive, expensive entertainment for the 'Welsh Toffs'. The large hand-out to refurbish Covent Garden was the last straw for the *Sun*, encouraging it to be even more vociferous on the Cardiff Bay scheme. On 22 December 1995 it could not hide its delight, and in front-page banner headlines gloated 'We've Won. No Lottery Cash for the Toffs!' The *Daily Mail* also produced a number of hostile and misleading stories.

In Cardiff the *Western Mail* and the *South Wales Echo* were much less consistent in their approaches. Jan Harris, in a perceptive article in the journal *Planet,* described the bewildering shifts of attitude revealed by their reports and leading articles. Immediately after the announcement of the competition winner, both newspapers portrayed Zaha Hadid's design in generally positive terms. The *Echo*, for example, ran an article comparing it to that of the Sydney Opera House, proclaiming its potential to become a landmark of equal stature – 'A Chorus of Approval' was the headline. The initial line was very quickly replaced by increasingly strident criticism, and by what Jan Harris describes as the two newspapers' 'butterfly approach', in which small reverberations – and there were many of these in the hectic weeks after the competition – were amplified into major objections. 'The rapid change of tone in the coverage of the *Western Mail* and to a lesser extent the *South Wales Echo* demonstrates this clearly', she comments. The early attempts to introduce and explain Hadid's design were quickly replaced by the build-up of a show-down scenario between Nicoletti and Hadid. The *Western Mail*, becoming intensely hostile to Hadid, portrayed itself as the public voice representing the will of the people. The paper's descriptions of the Hadid design became contemptuous. It was 'uninspiring', 'unattractive', a 'white elephant'. On 14 October 1994 there was the headline 'Albatross Necklace'; two months later it was: 'Doomed from the Beginning'. By February the following year the *Western Mail* was campaigning that 'Hadid's Design is the Wrong Choice.' Jan Harris holds the *Western Mail* responsible, more than any other party, for 'stirring up rancour' about the Opera House. It would no doubt argue that it was simply representing a widely held view. Certainly the *Echo* was never as hostile, although one of its regular columnists took a line similar to that of the *Sun*.

In the months that followed, both newspapers blew hot and cold, reacting to events and their readers' often wildly inaccurate comments. Among those events were the revised Hadid designs, my speech to the Cardiff Business Club and the alleged competition with the rugby ground. No newspaper can resist a competition, and in this instance they were determined to create one even if it was only in their imaginations.

Then came the most remarkable somersault of all, with the *Western Mail's* reaction to the decision of the Millennium

Commission. Conveniently forgetting the violent hostility it had shown such a short time before, it claimed that Hadid's design was 'not a folly, but a grand cultural adventure in the making'. Jan Harris comments:

> In the same issue the paper felt it necessary to present a summary of its own relationship with the troubled project under the heading 'the Rise and Fall of a Capital Dream' which omitted to mention the strength, and possibly decisive influence, of the paper's opposition, declaring that the *Western Mail* was convinced by the changes [to Hadid's design], and that not only would the crystal necklace work as a building but it would become a cultural icon for Wales in the world.

The paper which in February had declared that 'Hadid's Design is the Wrong Choice' (after the design changes had been made!) now produced an editorial which stated that 'Zaha Hadid's crystal necklace would have provided the platform for the world to perform in Wales'.

The announcement by the Millennium Commission of its rejection of the project seems to have taken most of the media by surprise. It was considered sufficiently astonishing for the *New York Times* to devote almost half of the front page of its Boxing Day edition to the subject. With few exceptions the press reacted with hostility and were vigorous in support of the Trust, Zaha Hadid and the project. The front pages of almost all the national papers on Saturday 23 December contained expressions of indignation. The *Western Mail* devoted huge space to an attack on the 'guilty' people, whom it identified as the Millennium commissioners, with their photographs across the front page, rather like a recent production of *Turandot* by WNO! They were accused of betraying Wales. The period of indignation was comparatively brief before the press picked up the more positive story that the Opera House project might be resurrected with the help of the National Museums and Galleries of Wales – to be followed all too soon by the story of the disastrous meeting at the museum and the winding up of the Trust soon after. All these events also received detailed coverage in Wales on television. HTV prepared a study of the project, filmed as events unfolded, and both HTV and BBC Wales offered to help the Trust with presentational material. The television reporting was throughout much more balanced and restrained than that of the more excitable sections of the press. Inevitably television producers could not resist the excitements of the opera–rugby clash; but even then, in general, the reporting and commentaries were reasonably balanced and fair.

The *Sun*'s anti-opera 'Toffs' headline after the project's rejection did more than demonstrate the fierce, irrational opposition to the Opera House project. It highlighted one of the central public-relations problems that confronted the Trust. From time to time public attitudes and politics become decisively influenced by a word or phrase that seems to represent a mood. To the *Sun* and presumably to many of its readers, 'opera' was a dirty word. It represented an extravagance that the 'rich' could enjoy, subsidized hugely from the taxpayer's pocket, a form of 'élitism' that was to be condemned. The two words 'opera' and 'élitism', which at another time and in another context might have signalled great artistic performance and excellence, came to represent indulgence and privilege, and joined a growing list of what is deemed to be politically incorrect.

The timing of the Arts Council of England's grant to the Royal Opera House could not have come at a worse time for the Cardiff project, which was caught in the backlash of hostile public opinion. Even in Wales, where Welsh National Opera was held in high esteem and attracts an audience which in general is probably less privileged and subsidized by business than that attending a rugby international at the Arms Park, the 'élitism' label stuck. Attempts to demonstrate that WNO was very unlike the Royal Opera were not successful. The Trust, through its public-relations programme, chipped away at this hard core of hostility, citing WNO's capacity to attract and delight many thousands of supporters from every sort of social background and income bracket, and the comparatively modest seat prices both in Cardiff and in the other theatres in Wales and England where the company toured. It also made much of the company's success as a breeding and training ground for great opera stars, some of whom proclaimed their support for the new Opera House. Perhaps the most powerful argument in support of 'opera for all' was Cardiff's happy experience of community productions, where local people with no opera background or training joined with WNO artists to present highly popular concerts in some of the most deprived parts of the city. The Trust, and in particular Alun Michael and Sue Harris, devoted an immense amount of effort to the development of community and education programmes intended to build on this well-established practice.

This particular difficulty might have been avoided but for the fatal mistake, made before the Trust existed, to call the building an opera house. Given his immense political experience and skill, it was a curious mistake for Peter Walker to have made, though I too should have spotted the danger and pressed for a change during the time when the Inkin committee was at work. The name was misleading and continued to cause people to misjudge the whole nature of the project right up to the end. This was not due to any lack of effort by the Trustees and their public-relations advisers. Hardly a day passed without the issue of a press hand-out, or a radio or television interview or speech, in which one or other representative repeated the message that three times as many people would come to the new building for musicals as would attend for opera, and that there would be dance and pantomime, and a range of exhibitions and community performances as well. It all had little effect, and to the very end there was widespread misunderstanding about the purpose and use to which the building was to be put. People sometimes express amazement that commercial organizations spend so much money on the selection of trading names and the design of logos. Here was a classic example of the devastating consequences if the name is wrong and the image misleading.

There was equally widespread misunderstanding about the nature of the lottery and the effect of the legislation that brought it into being, and anger over the delay in establishing the work programme of the Charities Board and in providing grants for charitable causes. The Trust was hit by the backlash from this tidal wave of public anger. The press were constantly publishing letters from irate readers demanding that instead of lottery millions going to opera houses and other causes which they did not favour, it should be spent on new hospitals and improving education. Trying to get across the fact that there was at that time no legal basis for Millennium Commission money to be spent on such causes seemed to be a waste of time. The arguments, for one reason or another, were simply not accepted.

Given this general atmosphere of hostility to some aspects of the lottery in the early months, and the wave of indignation about 'élitism', it was particularly unfortunate that the architectural selection should have been so controversial and that there should have been open disagreement about that selection among supporters of the project. Inevitably this combination created the kind of situation about which public-relations practitioners have bad dreams. The fact that the final choice was not unanimous, and the deliberate leaking of hostile views by individuals involved, made explosive copy for the press. It was much more fun reporting a good row than the virtues of the design or the importance of the project for Wales. The architects and the architectural press accused the Trust 'of panicking in the face of hostility', but as I wrote at the time, although 'you cannot sensibly choose an architectural team or a design by referendum or by television poll – for a project like this to succeed it really does need public goodwill'. Creating public goodwill in this situation was not easy.

A competition appeals to the press even more than a good row. When the Opera House project was first launched, there appeared to be no major competitor in Wales for the funds that the Millennium Commission was expected to produce for a dozen or so landmark schemes. The Welsh Rugby Union, working in close collaboration with Russell Goodway, the South Glamorgan County Council Labour leader, came on to the field comparatively late in the day. The plan was announced only a few weeks before applications had to be lodged with the Commission in the spring of 1995. WRU supporters campaigned on the basis that Wales could only have one really large project of this kind, and if the choice had to be made between rugby and opera it must be rugby. The Trust, which had from the start to contend with the negative arguments of those that disliked either opera, élitism, the design, or all three together, now had to contend as well with those who might not be against anything, but were very definitely in favour of rugby and the idea of building a new National Stadium.

The Trust took a firm decision not to get involved in a competitive dispute about the merits of the two schemes, although we could not help observing the curious fact that those who had been so passionately concerned about the design of an arts centre amid the new buildings arising in Cardiff Bay appeared to be entirely uninterested in the appearance of this enormous structure in the very heart of the city. There was no anonymous international competition to design the stadium, no public consultation and no furore about the fanciful drawings of hideous structures that were unveiled at the launch. It was always obvious that had there been a competition, the popular vote, stimulated by vigorous campaigning by the very numerous Welsh rugby clubs, would be likely to produce a majority in favour of rugby over the arts. We took a firm decision not to engage in a slanging match with the rugby supporters, but to express sympathy with their aspirations. With the assurance received from Virginia Bottomley, we were confident that it was possible for Wales to win both projects, and that the Commission would consider each on its merits. Rightly or wrongly, we decided not to mount any large-scale petition-type campaign, even though a more limited research project that we commissioned indicated very firm support in Wales for the Opera House.

Bob Skinner, in his report, criticized WNO for what he and some others believe was an inadequate public-relations campaign in favour of the Opera House. For WNO the construction of the Opera House was a key objective, and the company committed a great deal of time and resource to the project. The time spent on attending Trust meetings, in discussing locational and operational issues with the design team, and, above all, in fund-raising activity, was so substantial that on occasion it threatened the company's capacity to maintain its ordinary day-to-day activities. It was very clear to all of us involved that at every level WNO was totally committed, but despite this Bob Skinner believes that a priceless opportunity was lost to exploit WNO's great reputation as a public-relations tool. The basis of the criticism is that not enough was done to use the company's groundswell of support throughout Wales and in large parts of southern England. 'Very little publicity material produced by them was in any sense "hard sell" for their new home', writes Bob Skinner.

> The scores of thousands who made up their audience at their touring venues, including Cardiff's New Theatre, were not urged to join the army of supporters to send a bold signal to the Millennium Commission of the huge backing for the project. No space was found in their opera programmes for information on the Opera House or a plea to 'sign on' signifying their support . . . In my view the most glaring failure was not to capitalise on its 'captive audience', the many thousands who made up the audience for WNO's productions throughout and beyond Wales in

the months leading up to the application for Lottery funding . . .When confirmation of public support was cited by the Millennium Commission as one of the key elements in its consideration of any project, it seems in hindsight a tragedy that WNO's performance in contributing to the Trust's public relations campaign did not match the company's exciting, successful approach to presenting and marketing their own productions.

Looking back, with the benefit of the hindsight to which Bob Skinner alludes, it is odd. 'On the one occasion when a free concert was staged as part of the campaign outside the St David's Hall, there was an extraordinary public reaction. As Mandy Wix explained at the time,

> We talked to hundreds of shoppers and were absolutely overwhelmed by their support. With very rare exceptions they said, yes, they did want this marvellous new theatre built in Cardiff and that they would be there after it opened. In fact there was so much enthusiasm that people were running up to us wanting to buy tickets for the first shows.

If there was a failure, I and my fellow Trustees must share the blame, and I do not recall being asked by Bob Skinner to put this particular subject on the agenda for discussion.The truth is that we were all doing so much – and none more so than the representatives of WNO – that we did miss some opportunities and fail to do some things that might have been done.

I have referred elsewhere to the problem that we had in persuading Zaha Hadid of the need to produce attractive presentations of her design that ordinary people could understand. I have no doubt that our task in winning public approval would have been made a great deal easier if we had not been plagued by the exhibition model, and if we had from an early stage been able to produce the kind of illustrations that later swung opinion in our favour. The value of good-quality illustrative material was demonstrated at the launch of the design development in April 1995, but from then on there was an embarrassing absence of any further drawings until when, paradoxically, it was too late – a magnificent new model was completed just in time to be carried into the Commission's headquarters in London before they came to their decision. The lack of a model was not the fault of Zaha Hadid. Models are expensive, and this one could not be produced until the design work on which it was based had been done. The fact remains, however, that Mandy Wix and the public-relations team for many months had nothing new with which to convey to the public the exciting concept of the Opera House and how it was being developed. They had to make do with the early colour drawings and a few mini-sketches that were used in its posters.

It is tempting to judge the public-relations efforts of the Trust by the same criteria that one would use for a well-established and well-financed professional organization. We did not have the resources to organize things in that way, and had never contemplated that we would have to fight such vigorous campaigns in defence of the design and to protect the project from the hostility of the WRU and the press. Our small team in Cardiff did magnificent work despite these handicaps. The scale of what is involved in handling a high-profile project of this kind is illustrated by the fact that, in two days just before Christmas 1995, when the verdict of the Commission was known, Alun Michael and I gave more than thirty broadcasts for radio and television.

15   A Lack of Vision

I loved the design.
Virginia Bottomley at the Royal Academy

It is a pity that you did not love it enough.
Paul Koralek

At the press conference after the Millennium rejection of the project
I spoke of my despair at the lack of vision, leadership and courage
that today characterizes so many aspects of our national life. What
was particularly sad in this instance was that the people responsible
were not a group of minor officials or the representatives of some
lesser local authority, but included the Deputy Prime Minister and
the Secretary of State for National Heritage. It is very hard to believe
that, in a comparable situation, their Victorian or Edwardian
forebears would have missed the opportunity to erect this great
building and meet such an obvious and long-overdue social need. It is
equally hard to believe that French ministers and the members of a
similar commission in France would have failed in such an abject
way.

It was not just the final decision that was so regrettable, but also
the overall manner in which the Millennium Commission
approached its responsibilities. Its approach could not have been
more different from that of the Arts Councils and the National
Heritage Memorial Fund. That was a fact that we were in a
particularly strong position to verify, because so many of the
distinguished professionals who had been advising us had been
involved in, or had been acting as assessors for, other projects. The
Assessors' reports commissioned by the Arts Councils and the
National Heritage Memorial Fund were, as a matter of ordinary
practice, given to those being assessed and were discussed with them.
Considerable efforts were made by these funding bodies to overcome
obstacles and to find ways to achieve objectives which were easily
and naturally shared by men and women who had a clear vision of
the place of the arts in a civilized society, and of the opportunity
provided by the lottery. In contrast, our Cardiff Trust had not been

shown the assessment provided by a firm of accountants which the Commission used to defend their decision, even though we asked to see it. Even more surprising, the Commissioners were not shown, and apparently did not ask to see, the highly favourable assessments prepared by the distinguished experts appointed on the advice of the Arts Councils of England and Wales.

The Millennium Commission's approach, which will be painfully familiar to many who have had responsibility in the public sector, seems to have been based on the old-fashioned Civil Service view that the avoidance of blame is even more important than the avoidance of risk. For an organization also obsessed with the belief that any risks that did exist should be borne by others, this had a paralysing effect. In this age of the Private Finance Initiative (designed to encourage investment, together with a proper analysis and pricing of risk), Treasury attitudes have been changing, but these changes do not seem to have registered with the Commission. This may well have been a consequence of the unhappy decision that the Secretary of State for National Heritage should chair the Commission, and that its membership should also include another minister as well. The accounting officers in the department and the Commission may have had a perfectly natural inclination to concentrate on the need to protect their own backs and those of their ministers in the event of anything going wrong. It is an approach not best designed to cater for consideration of 'the bold and imaginative projects' which Virginia Bottomley had said she was seeking. In this sort of situation the problems are not there to be solved but are put to the bottom of the pile in the hope that they will go away.

Whenever the Cardiff Trustees asked for guidance on the key policy issues that were later to prove so important they received no response, and were always told that the Commission's initial set of rules could not be varied, even when common sense suggested that the results had not been foreseen. Richard Pulford had reported that 'the Opera House proposal represents by far the most significant landmark project yet to have emerged in the cultural sector in England and Wales' which 'fully warrants support from national lottery funds'; and yet a set of rules was operated that set an obstacle which would not have applied in England and which was used as an excuse for the scheme's disqualification. Later we were to have first the spectacle of Michael Heseltine standing proudly inside an Arms

Park which could have been very adequately modernized or replaced without any contribution from lottery money, and then an episode of ministerial arm-twisting in order to obtain funding for the Greenwich exhibition.

It seems clear that the aims of the Commission had changed since the time when Peter Brooke talked about twelve great projects, and that the Commission's interest became concentrated on worthy environmental schemes which did not invite press charges of élitism. It was unfortunate that this was not made plain much sooner. If it had been, it would have saved much effort, and prevented the waste of large sums of public and private money which had been invested in the expectation that the Millennium Commission really did want a lyric theatre in Cardiff which would contribute to economic and social regeneration in a challenging building worthy of the new millennium. One possible conclusion is that the project was shot down in flames by a combination of a controversial submission by the reporting accountants, which was at odds with a vast body of professional knowledge, experience and research; by the deplorable failure of the Commissioners to take proper account of the Arts Assessors; and by an opinion about the scale of the fund-raising gap largely created by their own unreasonable policy. However, some people believe that there is an even simpler explanation, and that the Commission caved in as a result of a populist clamour against élitism and the hostility of the *Sun* newspaper. It is suggested that a political decision was taken that, after previous rows, the easy way out would be to sacrifice the Welsh. It is not a view that is flattering to the Commissioners, but something changed at the last moment, and so many different explanations have been offered by Commission spokesmen that such speculation is inevitable.

At a Dorset wedding nine months after the event, Virginia Bottomley informed me and a former Cabinet minister that she had struggled single-handed for a week to save a project which she favoured, but that none of her colleagues would support her. She complained of the injustice of politics, which forced her to announce and defend a decision that she regretted. Assuming that this is the case, it is remarkable that a chairman who was also Minister for National Heritage had so little influence; and it still does not provide an explanation for the fact that two Commissioners who had always been enthusiastic supporters should have apparently withdrawn their backing. Another version of what happened is that Sir John Hall proved hostile and influenced Michael Heseltine, a combination of powerful personalities that could not be resisted. Surely Michael Heseltine must have played a key role. If he and Virginia Bottomley had supported the project I find it hard to believe that it would not have been approved.

A leading Labour politician told me that it was his opinion that if Peter Walker, David Hunt or I had been at the Welsh Office we would not have allowed it to happen. I think that is a rather tough verdict on William Hague, who was new to office and hardly in a position to challenge two senior colleagues once the die was cast. However, I think that there is some truth in the judgement that the Welsh Office could have been much more proactive in ensuring the right result and a good return on the sum of over £2 million that it had invested. It could have done a number of things. It could have made it impossible for Jennifer Page to claim lack of support from the Welsh Office. It could, before the Commission met in December 1995, have announced a favourable decision on our bid for a £12 million European grant. It could, without spending anything like the sum originally asked for by the Inkin committee or the sum that I had found in 1986 for the National Museum, have removed the need for us to bid for Millennium funds for WNO accommodation or car parking. At the very least, it could have urged the importance of the project on the Commission. It seems that the Welsh Office sat inactive on the sidelines, although less than a year later we had the curious spectacle of the Secretary of State inviting Welsh business-men to lunch in order to seek their support for the Millennium Exhibition in Greenwich. Clearly priorities had changed since my time there. It may be that some Redwood attitudes still lingered, or that the drip-drip of hostility from within the CBDC had a negative impact, or that the fierce hostility to Hadid shown by Michael Scholar at that meeting in Gwydyr House lingered on and influenced the advice he gave, despite the sympathetic words that he uttered to me. Certainly the Welsh Office stood back when clear-cut support was most needed, and it must, therefore, share some part of the blame for this major set-back to its policies, and for the loss of the public money that it had committed.

Did the press play a decisive part? It was important but, on its own, not decisive in my judgement, despite the extraordinary coverage of the drama from beginning to end. This coverage may, it is true, have sown the seeds of doubt in some minds; but is unlikely that that would have been enough if the CBDC and the local authorities had behaved differently. Its impact was not so much on the Commission but upon the climate of opinion in Wales. It helped to encourage that ever-present tendency of my fellow countrymen to fight among themselves; it built up the belief that a choice had to be made between the Opera House and the rugby ground; and it added substantially to the difficulties that the Trustees and our fund-raising teams had to overcome.

When, as Secretary of State, I set up the CBDC and invited Geoffrey Inkin to be its chairman I was careful to leave planning powers with the local authorities. I was determined to avoid the tensions that had been created by a different policy in the early life of London Docklands. The Cardiff City Council was therefore the authority to whom we would have had to submit a planning application if our Millennium bid had succeeded in 1995. We had taken a good deal of trouble to keep the City Council informed of our developing plans and had their assurance that they would not see any value in seeking to second-guess the judgement of the Trustees on the choice of design and architect, so that we did not foresee serious planning difficulties. The CBDC did have the job of preparing the structure plan and setting high standards of design. Before the Opera House became a matter of controversy, I wrote the comment that they sometimes 'seemed to be more concerned with preparing beautiful plans than in achieving real development'. On this occasion they became so preoccupied with their architectural obsessions that they were prepared to put at risk one of their central objectives of policy, a point made clear by the apparently triumphant way in which their chief executive broke the news to one leading figure in the Cardiff arts world on the day that our rejection became public.

I was guilty of one serious error in my handling of the whole business. At the time it was decided that there should be a separate trust to manage the project, I should have strongly recommended that the responsibilities of the two organizations should be clearly defined, so that there could be no question of the Corporation seeking to do the Trust's work for it or, worse, in conflict with it. After the row had broken, and seeing the CBDC rampaging around, I should have refused to become chairman until a way had been found of resolving this potentially disastrous situation. I suppose that, having created the organization and appointed its chairman, I was lulled into the belief that any potential difficulties could be overcome by the use of well- established personal relationships. I was very soon to be sharply disillusioned.

The approach adopted by the Corporation appears to have had a seriously damaging impact on the Commission's perception of the project and on the attitude of the Welsh Office, with whom Geoffrey Inkin was in very frequent contact. It also sowed the seeds of distrust about the conduct of the CBDC within the Trust and those who worked for it, which made working relationships more difficult. There was a period, after Hadid's appointment had been confirmed and before the Commission rejection, when we stumbled forward in an uneasy relationship as Inkin attempted with some success to control the more outspoken opponents within the CBDC and provide us with the funds that we required. They were persuaded that their position would be impossible to defend and that they would suffer all the blame if they pulled the rug from under us while we prepared to face the Commission. With the Commission decision taken, they could hardly wait to finish us off, and were clearly surprised and irritated that we refused to die and actually came forward with a serious revision of the original proposal.

That the chairman decided to terminate any further consideration of the Hadid scheme or proper discussion of the options without any consultation with us, and in a way that prevented a proper considera-tion of the issues at a meeting arranged with much care by the Institute of Welsh Affairs, can hardly be presented simply as an error of judgement. Others not involved may take a more charitable view, but writing long after the event I still find it hard to excuse or forgive.

I have frequently asked myself whether the Trust could have changed the outcome by doing things differently after taking over the responsibility from the Inkin committee which had set the initial course. Try as I may, I cannot think of anything significant we could reasonably have done that was not done. There had been an international competition that attracted a large number of entries and international interest. The architect was selected after an immensely thorough testing of the design and the capacity of her team. We had put in place project-management and fund-raising teams of world class. We had sought advice from the very best people in the world of music, opera and theatre. We had a Trust membership that should itself have been an adequate guarantee of expertise and quality.

There were some things that might have been done differently. I have already identified the failure to ensure that there was a clear separation of the roles of the Trust and our funding body. I believe that the decision we took in the Inkin committee to have four short-listed architects and two rounds of the competition proved to be a mistake. The Assessors should have met with the short-listed architects as we had intended when the rules were drawn up. It would have been better if the chairman of the Trust had not also been the chairman of the Assessors. The objective of putting the same person in both positions had been to reduce the risk of damaging disagreements. The decision to do so having been taken, the principle should have been taken to its logical conclusion, and the Assessors, the Trustees, and the 'attendees' (Geoffrey Inkin and I) should have sat down together to see if an agreed position could be reached before a public announcement was made which would have enabled all the parties to go forward in complete unity. The outcome of the competition might well have been the same, and later events suggest that it would have been; but if we had been able to speak with one voice everything that followed might have been different.

One person closely involved has suggested that the Trustees' task would have been much easier if the competition rules had required the Assessors to select three or four designs and award prizes, while making it clear that the Trust would then enter into a more thorough process of examination and negotiation with each of the prizewinners before making the final appointment. This would have enabled the Trust to protect its own position, given legitimacy to a process that in the event took place anyway and made it easier to inform and consult the public. Some architects might be very reluctant to enter a competition of that kind; but, unless something of the kind is done in the future, the Cardiff experience may have put paid to the large-scale architectural competition as a method of selection in the United Kingdom for some time to come. The 'restricted procedure' route where architects are invited to pre-qualify, and then a much smaller group are invited to submit proposals, now seems to be the favoured method, but it is an approach that makes it more difficult for outsiders or the talented young to make their mark. What is certain is that the method of public consultation attempted in Cardiff did not work to anyone's advantage. If there was to be some public consultation before the winner of the competition was announced – and I am far from convinced that consultation at that stage in the proceedings could have been meaningful – then clearly the few hours of the third symposium were inadequate.

The structure of the competition was settled and some of those mistakes were made before the Trust took over its responsibilities, and it is therefore tempting for those involved only in the later stages to put the blame largely on the shortcomings of the competition procedures; but I am doubtful if the controversy could have been avoided, even if the changes that I now suggest with the benefit of hindsight had been made at the time.

I have a feeling that there were those, and perhaps Geoffrey Inkin was among them, who thought that I was taking on the chairmanship in the middle of the monumental row that developed in order to play a much more Machiavellian role than I ever contemplated, a role that would have involved ruthlessly discarding Zaha Hadid in order to defuse the row and achieve unity in Wales speedily. That was never a realistic possibility because I held the old-fashioned view that Zaha Hadid, having won a major competition, was entitled to be treated fairly. In any case, I doubt whether my fellow Trustees could have been persuaded to be parties to any such deal. It is also highly improbable that it could have been made to work. There would have been an immense row in the architectural world, and no guarantee that it would have been adequately offset by the achievement of a new unity of purpose in Cardiff.

While it is right to be self-critical when failure is the outcome of one's efforts, and to acknowledge the possibility that it might have been possible to do some things differently, my firm conclusion is that the achievements of the Trust, its employees and its professional advisers were remarkable. If we had been allowed to proceed we should have produced a building that would have been world-famous and met all the original objectives of the Inkin committee, the Arts Council of Wales and the Cardiff Bay Development Corporation. We had brought together some of the finest professionals in the world to ensure that in functional terms it would work superbly, and that it would be constructed on time and within our budgets. We had assembled a team of fund-raisers of comparable quality. The knowledge and experience of our own Trustees, together with the detailed professional analysis that we had carried out across the whole spectrum of performing-arts organizations in this country, but also including many abroad, should have provided more than adequate assurance of the commercial viability of the project in the future. The design received the enthusiastic blessing of the Royal Fine Arts Commission. The planning authority indicated that it would not seek to second-guess the Trust and the Assessors.

Against this background all of us involved have speculated about what was the real cause of our downfall. Adrian Ellis tells me that Simon Jenkins, himself a Millennium commissioner, wrote somewhere that politics always trumps economics, and he suggests that the stuff about the business plan was a sideshow. In one sense I suppose that he is right: it was not BDO Stoy Haward, those reputable accountants who saw it as their proper duty to identify every conceivable risk, that decided our fate, or even the unrealistic view taken by Commission officials that the design phase of this large building should be virtually complete and almost all the private money raised before they would recommend that any lottery funds should be committed. It is a proper function of accountants and officials to identify possible risks; it is the responsibility of those that employ them to decide whether or not the assessments are realistic and the risks significant. Anyone who has been a minister or observed the process of government closely will know that, however good civil servants and professional consultants may be, the major influence that decides whether or not things happen is the attitude of ministers. If ministers know what they want, civil servants are good at bringing it about. If ministers do not know what they want, or lack the ability to take decisions, then things simply do not happen or events overwhelm them. The same principle applies equally to organizations like the Millennium Commission. It is of course true that ministers and those who are in charge of such organizations will react to public opinion and to the advice that they receive, but if they have clear objectives they will do what is required to influence what others think, and will see that the sails are trimmed to ensure that the objective is achieved.

It seems doubtful whether the Millennium Commissioners ever had a certain and single-minded purpose that they could convey to those who worked for them. If they had, they failed to make it clear to the world outside. The Commission found itself with an event to celebrate, a lot of money, several thousand suggestions about how it should be spent and a series of chairmen with numerous other responsibilities. Events seem to have dictated the course that it followed. Apparently the Commission did form a view about some things that they should not be doing: they were anxious not to duplicate the work of the Charities Board, the Arts Councils and the National Heritage Memorial Fund, all of which did have clear objectives (although the Charities Board took an exceedingly long time to decide what they were – which had a damaging impact on public opinion). Initially it seemed that the Commission, under its first chairman, would want to celebrate the millennium with a dozen or so really substantial projects which would surely include important architectural commissions of a kind with which earlier generations had celebrated great events. There seemed a chance that we would leave for our children an inheritance comparable to the great complex of cultural buildings in Kensington constructed after the Great Exhibition. That idea was apparently soon abandoned, and instead it seems that the Commission had decided that the millennium is to be celebrated in Britain by hundreds of worthy local projects, an exhibition at Greenwich, and a number of larger environmental schemes (all of which at least appear virtuous compared with the ghastly Ferris wheel that some people wish to erect on the banks of the Thames). The commissioners also seem to have formed the view that risks could be taken with environmental schemes, such as the Earth Centre near Doncaster or the Welsh Botanic Garden in west Wales, which were thought unacceptable in the case of our project in Cardiff. Perhaps they believed that the public would be sympathetic and not too critical if the funding failed to materialize or the assumptions on which the business plans were based proved too optimistic.

I visited the Earth Centre with the board of the National Rivers Authority soon after its grant had been announced. While I was delighted by the prospect that the dereliction in a once-beautiful river valley might be removed and an interesting exhibition complex constructed on its banks, I was relieved that I did not have the responsibility of bringing this very substantial project to a successful conclusion, or of maintaining the flow of visitors required if it was to be viable. My reaction to the Welsh Botanic Garden was very similar. I hope that it is a success, but I shall be pleasantly surprised if the visitor numbers that have been forecast are achieved. I find it difficult to understand how the Commission could have greater confidence in the forecasts made in this instance than those that were included in our bid, based as they were on a wealth of information and the experience of many analogous arts centres in other cities in Britain and around the world. I have no criticism to make of the Commission's desire to promote bold environmental schemes. I think it should be prepared to take risks and, at the very least, join as a genuine partner in the risk business. What requires explanation is the fact that the Commission appears to have followed two different policies simultaneously: accepting clear and obvious risks for environmental projects, but rejecting the Cardiff application on the grounds that there were too many uncertainties.

It is significant that the policy of the Commission appears to have changed as successive Secretaries of State took up their posts and their position as chairman of the Commission. Given the membership of the Commission, it is not surprising that there was a lack of simple, clear and bold objectives, or that the approach of the Secretary of State was to prove so important. The character of the Commission has been influenced by the fact that the members are not only different in background, interest, political opinion and experience, but they are all very busy people. We gained the impression that important material in our submission was never read by officials; whether that is a correct judgement or not, it seems certain that only a very small part of it will have been examined by very busy commissioners who have had to consider and pass judgement on a huge number of applications. In this situation two factors are likely to have had a decisive impact. The first is the nature of the advice submitted by Jennifer Page, her officials and her consultants. The second factor was political, or perhaps it can best be described as just plain funk. A Commission with no clear ambition to produce even a handful of great buildings, and with an inadequate understanding of the project, seemed to have been panicked by the public reaction to the Arts Council grant for the Royal Opera House, by all the nonsense about élitism and above all by the noise of the 'ferrets fighting in a sack' in Cardiff. The noise of those ferrets must have been very alarming to the rabbits sitting nervously in Little Smith Street. The high-pitched screaming of the local politicians and the board of the CBDC must have seemed even louder because of the remarkable silence of the Welsh MPs close by in Westminster. Perhaps it was the old feud between the Valley communities and those who live in the capital city on the plain that caused some of those MPs to be silent when their support was so badly needed.

A situation was created in which negative influences were almost bound to dominate and to overwhelm all our carefully constructed reports, the professional skills and expertise of the design team and our advisers, the numerous studies about need and viability, the detailed financial planning and the expertise of the Trustees. A commissioner sees headlines about public hostility to the design, hears that Cardiff councillors want a rugby ground and not an opera house, and is told that even the CBDC and the Welsh Office are not enthusiastic; suddenly it seems much easier to lead a quiet life and give money for seed banks, bicycle tracks and coastal parks. It may not be very exciting, but at least it seems safe and uncontroversial.

All sorts of rumours swept Cardiff in the weeks that followed the decision: it was the result of a direct order from No. 10; it came from prejudice because Zaha Hadid is a woman, and an Iraqi at that; the Commissioners hated the design. I do not believe any of these rumours, but I do know that fear is perhaps the most significant of all political realities, and leadership combined with vision is required to overcome it. Virginia Bottomley has many admirable qualities, but she is no Prince Albert.

So in the end the verdict must be reached that politics and dissension were decisive. Conflicts in Cardiff, a critical press, a controversial design, the name Opera House given to the building, an absurd hostility to opera on the grounds that it is élitist, an inadequate and superficial knowledge of the project by the Commissioners and, perhaps above all, a lack of vision, courage and leadership by those with the greatest responsibilities: all these produced a disaster for the arts in Britain and the people of Wales, and a personal tragedy for Zaha Hadid.

16   Postscript: Wales Millennium Centre

This new venue will provide something for everyone – *it will offer all kinds of shows, world-class entertainments and exhibitions nearly every day of the year.*
Cardiff Bay Opera House publicity material

This exciting and innovative Complex has been specifically designed not only to stage a wide variety of art forms with top quality acoustics, but also to become a major attraction for both visitors and the people of Wales.
Wales Millennium Centre publicity material

After the disastrous meeting at the National Museum many of us involved in the Opera House bid believed that there should be a pause before further action was taken. There was too much mutual distrust in Cardiff to give confidence that sensible fresh proposals could be formulated; and there were few reasons to think that any new scheme that met the objectives that the Trust had shared with the Inkin committee could have a significantly different business plan or be achieved at a much lower cost than the Hadid scheme. Lottery funding would continue to be available beyond the millennium and perhaps it would be better to wait until the Millennium Commission had handed over its responsibilities to other funding bodies. At that stage the CBDC would also have come to the end of its appointed term; and it was even possible that the attitudes of those who controlled local government in Cardiff might have changed for the better. In any case we were sickened by what had happened, and had no stomach for a renewal of the struggle. We therefore began the process of winding up the Trust. Others thought differently. They included those who had so bitterly opposed Hadid, but also David Davies and Anthony Freud of WNO, desperate because the company might soon be without a home; and officers of the National Museum, impatient to get on with its long-delayed plans. Members of the Institute of Welsh Affairs and the local press also thought that there was an opportunity that should not be missed. So it was that, a very short time after the assassination of the Hadid scheme, a new initiative was launched. In these circumstances it was a peculiar irony that only a few months later, in the autumn of 1996, Mathew Prichard, the original chairman of the Opera House Trust, should have become president of the Museum following the sad death of my brother Tim, and was thus plunged back into the saga.

Ann had been deeply shocked by the events of 8 March and by the letters dispatched that day by the chairman of the CBDC. Her gut instinct was that a new home for WNO would be better placed outside the Bay area; and she warned David Davies that she might resign from the Board of the company if he and Anthony Freud decided to rush into a hastily cobbled-together new scheme on the same site. She had been a member of the Welsh Arts Council during the 1980s and had been involved in all the early studies. She was terrified that the company might jump out of the frying-pan and into the fire.

In the month that followed she sought out possible sites eligible for Heritage lottery money that might at least give WNO office and rehearsal space. She invited Colin Ford, the director of the Museum, and his wife Sue to lunch to meet Lindsay Evans, the Welsh trustee of the National Heritage Memorial Fund and Heritage Lottery Fund, to hear about the Museum's plans and to tap Lindsay's vast knowledge of Welsh historic buildings, arising from his many years of service on the Welsh Historic Buildings Council. Both men proposed a number of buildings that might be a possible home for WNO in the short term.

It was a hectic time for everyone at WNO. The company was preparing for its fiftieth anniversary concert in St David's Hall on 20 April which was a huge success. It was during this celebratory weekend, when so many were gathered in Cardiff, that Ann began to realize how little her English Board colleagues knew about the demise of the opera house project. On Welsh TV and in the Welsh newspapers there had been reports about the meeting at the Museum and the fateful letters; but little of this information had percolated to Birmingham and beyond.

At a Board meeting of WNO on 22 April David Davies and Anthony Freud gave an oral report and outlined the features of a possible new plan for a performing arts centre on the same site in the Bay. Although they were in possession of very little information about it, the Board gave their approval for further exploratory work to be carried out. Ann arrived back in London in tears, feeling that she must resign. I begged her not to, and she flew to Egypt the next day for a short holiday having agreed to ponder the matter. When she returned in high spirits to our home in Wales an event occurred that was to prove the final straw. My brother Tim, the president of the Museum, rang to say that a friend had telephoned to ask him to alert Ann to the fact that, at a meeting about the new project in London on Friday 4 May, one of those attending had threatened legal action against her if she continued to voice the criticisms that presumably had percolated beyond the privacy of the WNO Board. Faced by unpleasantness on this scale, and anxious not to embarrass colleagues at WNO or Tim in his role as president, she rang David Davies and resigned from the Board. Deeply attached to the company, she has continued enthusiastically to help the development department and give support from outside.

When the new initiative was launched, I was surprised that so little advantage was taken of the material that we had accumulated and the experience that we had gained. I was not surprised, however, that the Cardiff office of Ove Arup took a leading role: they had approached our Trust early in 1996 with a proposal that if progress with the Hadid scheme became impossible we should make use of the design on which they had been working for a temporary home near Tower Bridge in London for the Royal Opera House. The project had been abandoned and they were anxious that the work should not be wasted. In any case, such is the range of their relevant experience that their participation in a project of this kind is almost inevitable regardless of the choice of architect.

More surprising and open to criticism was the decision of the Percy Thomas Partnership, which had entered into 'a healthy long-term relationship' with the Office of Zaha Hadid, to put their name forward for the limited selection process that was now undertaken by the organizers to find her successor. The announcement of their appointment created well-justified unhappiness and adverse comment among architects and others, not because there were any doubts about their competence, but because of the nature of the previous partnership with Zaha Hadid. The method of selection chosen on this occasion was for those involved to interview a limited number of architects and then to make a selection on the basis of the ideas put forward. The design would emerge later and the public's opportunity to be involved in the process would be minimal. When eventually the sketches of an outline scheme did emerge and later a model was produced, the public – perhaps exhausted by its previous excitement – showed remarkably little interest.

The small group involved, in which Freddy Watson initially played the leading role, was greatly strengthened when Sir Alan Cox, recently retired as managing director of Allied Steel and Wire, agreed to take the chair. In addition to Freddy Watson, his colleagues were David Davies (chairman of WNO), Roger Thomas (council member of the National Museums and Galleries), Jim Beveridge (board member of the CBDC) and David Jenkins (secretary of the Wales TUC). The CBDC provided staff and office facilities. The project managers were Gleeds; the architects were the Percy Thomas Partnership. Ove Arup were the structural engineers and acousticians, Symonds the quantity surveyors; Carr and Angier, who had been consultants to the Welsh Arts Council a decade previously, returned as theatre consultants. Those involved were faced with some quite severe problems, not the least of which was shortage of funds and time. In a letter to me Virginia Bottomley confirmed that the requirements of the Millennium Commission would be the same as before; the design would have to be developed to RIBA Stage C with a 5–10 per cent contingency; there would have to be evidence of the capacity to raise matching funds, and to do so in a way that triggered parallel funding from the lottery; and there would have to be an adequate business plan that included acceptable expenditure and revenue projections.

Sir Keith Stuart on behalf of ABP offered similar support to that previously advanced to the Trust, with the primary object of helping WNO. Much more would be needed for the expensive design work required for this large and complex scheme. Money would have to be found once again to do what had already been done before. However, on this occasion the lottery funding bodies were prepared to help with this preliminary work. The decision whether or not the project would be short-listed for further consideration was originally to be made in January 1997 and the final decision taken just a few months later. Russell Goodway and the Cardiff County Council at that critical stage were still avoiding any form of financial commitment; they complicated the business still further by submitting a £20 million bid to the Millennium Commission for a quite different project for the improvement of the river frontage of the Taff and for

leisure facilities along its banks between the city centre and Cardiff
Bay. The Commission decided that the Millennium Centre would go
forward for further consideration, but the river frontage scheme was
rejected. The backers of the Millennium Centre project were now
faced with a further long period of expense and uncertainty, with a
decision postponed until late in the year, by which time a general
election would have led to changes in the leadership and ministerial
membership of the Commission.

In two substantial respects things were made easier. This time the
principal players were not being sent in to bat with broken bats, to
use Geoffrey Howe's now famous analogy; and the lottery funding
was now to be shared with the Heritage Lottery Fund and the Arts
Council of Wales. These bodies were expected to be more positive in
their approach and to be willing to produce 75 per cent or more of
the cost of those parts of the building to be used by the Museum and
WNO. In April, however, National Heritage Memorial Fund staff
responsible for the Heritage Lottery Fund began to express doubts
about their readiness to help finance the IMAX cinema which was
central to the Museum's plans. At about the same time substantial
changes were being made to the design, with the removal of the
proposed rear wing of offices and the original projecting restaurant.

In this situation, and with the need to gather public support, it is
not surprising that the organizers found it necessary to produce a
myth. The public was told that this was an entirely different project.
Not only had the architect changed, they said, but the aims were
quite different. Unlike the Opera House, the Millennium Centre –
they had adopted the kind of name that I had proposed more than a
year before and which the Opera House Trust had formally
embraced at its February meeting – was not going to be 'élitist', but a
'people's palace' to provide populist entertainment.

The trouble with that presentation was that it was incorrect. The
brief was still the same and the proposed content of the building
(except for the possible inclusion of a commercial wing, later
discarded, and a youth centre for the Urdd, the Welsh youth
movement) was exactly as it had been when Hadid and the Trust had
been stabbed in the back. The auditorium was to accommodate
between 1,700 and 2,000; there was to be a wing for the Museum and
an IMAX cinema; there would be facilities for exhibitions and
performances by a variety of organizations, space in the open for

entertainment, accommodation for WNO and a restaurant with views over the Bay. The use to which these facilities were to be put was also unchanged, with the same balance between popular musicals and opera, the same kind of museum, and the same attractions to draw people in. Alun Michael's unconsidered paper for the abortive meeting at the Museum proposed nothing that differed in a material respect from what was now offered by the promoters as being something entirely new. I attach no blame. The organizers had presumably come to the same conclusion as I had: that the previous rejection was political and that they therefore had to use political guile if they were to have any prospect of success.

I am critical of their repeated statements that what made this building different was that, unlike Hadid's, it was designed from the inside out; that the exterior design was secondary and evolved from what was to happen inside. I have described earlier in this book how Hadid's building evolved in exactly that way, though firmly rooted in the urban context. We were also told that the team was not 'architect-led'. It is a comment that does not exactly flatter the architects, unless it merely states the truth that good architecture springs from a partnership between architect and client, and that it is the client who decides the building's purpose. It occurred to me that it might mean that this was a design that sprang from material already available, and that use was being made of work already done. The trouble with even the best myths is that they leave matters uncertain and tend as a result to become embroidered.

It was not, however, the design that confronted the sponsors with their greatest difficulty, but the business plan. Despite the substantial research that had been done over a whole decade, and the expertise that we had available, our business plan had been criticized and made the excuse for our rejection. BDO Stoy Haward had given us their own apocalyptic version. Even without their pessimism, it is absolutely certain that the new plan cannot offer significantly greater security and certainty than the old. Sharing costs with the Museum may provide some benefits over our original project, although not over our revised scheme involving the Museum; but Museums do not usually make money, and in the theatre similar shows are to be put on. The managers of this 'people's palace' cannot intend to charge more for the seats. To a significant extent the new business plan will provide less security. We budgeted, conservatively, for a possible loss and determined to raise an endowment fund to cover it. For the new scheme there is to be no endowment, and the local authority has refused to step in to fill the gap. It will be interesting to see what the Commission's financial appraisal makes of this. If they do back the project it will be clear that the criticism of the Cardiff Bay Opera House Trust's business plan was no more than a smoke-screen, and that the decision to reject our bid was largely political. It remains unclear who will bear the risk of an operating loss at the Millennium Centre.

Michael Heseltine had complained of the cost of our proposals and said that this was the principal obstacle. Well, he and others can now forget the nonsense about coming back with a scheme costing no more than the Manchester concert hall. At the 'outline planning stage' the total bid for the new Millennium Centre was already £86 million, and the direct capital spend £72 million, excluding infrastructure and land (and £4 million for separate arts facilities in Cardiff). Whether these costs will stay the same when the design is taken to a more advanced stage, and whether the lottery funding bodies judge that the inflation assumption and contingencies are adequate, remains to be seen. Even if the inclusion of the Museum wing in the Hadid building (partially offset by the removal of car parking) had led to some further increase in the December 1995 figure, it is clear that the costs of the two schemes are not going to be very far apart. The Opera House Trust was also raising £7 million to cover the possible operating deficit.

The involvement of the other lottery funding bodies was expected to reduce the scale of the private-sector capital funding requirement. The organizers hoped that the Heritage Lottery Fund would provide a substantial proportion of the cost of the Museum facility: press articles reported a figure of £18 million. A figure of £6 million was sought from the Arts Council of Wales, leaving £27 million from the Millennium Commission, a total of £51 million compared with the £50 million that we were asking for. However, even with some optimistic assumptions about European funding and about any sums that might be raised by the Museum and WNO from land disposal, the fund-raising task is very clearly not going to be easy, particularly if the final design turns out not to be of a kind that attracts the exceptional giver.

Initial reactions to the design were less than enthusiastic. Before I saw the first sketches, the representative of one leading architectural journal described it as an 'appalling mess, a conglomeration of borrowed references from other architects – almost a cartoon of "spot the architect". There is nothing', he said, 'that refers to the site, to Cardiff, or that indicates original thinking.' Rowan Moore, writing in an article in *The Daily Telegraph* under the heading 'How Not to Build an Opera House', made the comment that it was just as well that the Percy Thomas Partnership called their sketches 'conceptual drawings': 'if they were real designs they would be a risible confection of current architectural cliché'. It was probably unkind to make such harsh judgements on the basis of preliminary sketches. At least when a model was produced, the hideous rooftop restaurant, apparently copied from the RAC's control room sited beside the M5 at Bristol, had been altered and replaced.

The remarkable fact about public reaction to the design when the first model was shown was that it was very low-key; that no doubt was exactly what the sponsors wanted. If the design did not arouse any enthusiasm, it did not provoke hostility either. The first impression of the building as viewed by those approaching from the city was of a rather dull curved wall of the Museum wing flanked by a feeble arch, which revealed but hardly improved the view of the far more robust Victorian Pierhead Building. The arch and the rooftop restaurant to which it was attached were later removed; and at the time of writing this book, other changes were still being made. It seems unlikely, however, that they will be so substantial as to alter the initial verdict. The new design prompts memories of dozens of arts centres in provincial cities around the world. One Assessor observed to me that there were twenty or thirty similar designs among the entries for the Opera House competition. It is not the world-class building by a world-class architect for which some had asked. It will not present a vivid image for Cardiff, except perhaps of decent respectability. Perhaps that is no bad thing. While very few outsiders will come to Wales with the primary object of seeing it, it may adequately serve its purpose, and the people of Wales certainly do deserve a building in which they can enjoy a musical. Welsh National Opera does deserve a proper home. There is a need for a performing-arts centre in the capital city and a focus for the great regeneration project that is under way in Cardiff Bay.

The arrival of a new government and a new chairman of the Millennium Commission may provide an opportunity and an excuse to change rules and eliminate obstacles. If the lottery funders now take the political decision to throw aside their previous criteria and back the project, then a great many local people will, I am certain, use and enjoy the facilities that it will offer. I hope it may be built; if it is, like many others, I will visit it, not because I am likely to be thrilled by its architecture but because I will want to enjoy yet another great performance by Welsh National Opera or some other worthwhile show. That is not to say that I shall be content. This Millennium Centre may be a completely appropriate memorial for those responsible for it, but Wales and the world deserved better. I shall never be able to look at it without regret at the opportunity that was missed, and without thinking of Zaha Hadid and the great and dramatic building that could have stood there in Cardiff Bay.

Epilogue

In the time that has elapsed since the conclusion of the events described in this book some of the principal players have moved to perform other roles. Virginia Bottomley ceased to be Secretary of State for National Heritage and chairman of the Millennium Commission as a consequence of the 1997 general election and was replaced by Chris Smith. In a curious switch of responsibilities, Jennifer Page moved from the Millennium Commission to be chief executive of the Millennium Exhibition, which was subsequently relaunched as the Millennium Experience. Peter Mandelson, Minister without Portfolio, unveiling the revamped plans on 26 June 1997, claimed that it was a chance that should not be missed to inspire the nation with 'the most thrilling experience on the planet'. The cost of the project was raised to £750 million, of which £400 million was to come from the lottery.

Only days before the decision to back the Greenwich celebration was announced by the Prime Minister, the Millennium Commission rejected a lottery bid for the latest of a number of possible schemes designed to rescue Stonehenge from the twin assaults of modern traffic and tourism. By this decision, the Commission incurred the wrath of Jocelyn Stevens, the chairman of English Heritage. His pithy comments indicated that his experience with the Commission had been very similar to our own.

As a result of all these events and the curious policies that have been followed, we are to celebrate the millennium with what the government's principal 'spin doctor', but very few others, thinks will be 'the most thrilling experience on the planet', under a temporary dome for which no longer-term purpose has been proposed, having cast on one side the only really significant architectural project to have emerged as a result of the lottery and rejected a unique opportunity to do justice to the greatest prehistoric monument in Britain. Two thousand years of history and Christianity are to be celebrated with an orgiastic experience. Some may feel that this exactly represents the current decadence of our society. My own view is that it is neither representative nor worthy; but that we have been let down, and we have failed both the generation that has brought us to the millennium and those that will inherit what we will leave behind.

Index

University of Wales, Cardiff, formerly
   University of Wales College of
   Cardiff 4
Urdd (Urdd Gobaith Cymru) 84, 165
Utzon, Jorn 26,

Visitor Centre, Cardiff Bay 77
Vitra fire station, Weil am Rhein 62

Wales Millennium Centre 161, 165,
   167–9,
Wales Tourist Board 130
Wales TUC 164
Walker, Peter (Lord Walker of
   Worcester) 7, 8, 9, 144, 152
Watson, Freddy 18, 19, 22, 35, 36, 164
Welsh Arts Council 1, 8, 14, 19, *see
   also* Arts Council of Wales
Welsh Development Agency 130
Welsh National Opera 1, 2, 5, 6–8, 10,
   15, 17, 19, 34, 35, 37, 38, 40, 42, 43,
   49, 50, 67, 72, 75, 77, 79, 82, 85,

90–2, 95, 106, 108, 110, 116, 118,
   119, 120, 122, 124, 126, 130, 133,
   134–6, 138, 143, 146, 147, 152, 161
   162–6, 167, 168, 169
Welsh Office 1, 3, 4, 7, 8, 9, 10, 11, 14,
   25, 41, 54, 56, 67, 71, 152, 154, 160,
Welsh Rugby Union 69, 70, 86, 129,
   138, 140, 143, 145, 148
Western Mail 22, 53, 58, 68, 69, 70, 71,
   86, 87, 114, 120, 129, 138, 141, 142
Weston, Doug 83, 116–17
Weston, Jo 76
Wigley, Dafydd 95
Wilford, Michael 18
Wilkinson, Heather 76, 77, 115, 117
Williams, David 19, 29, 112
Williams, Huw 5, 48
Williams, Kyffin 89
Wix, Mandy 5, 31, 59, 75, 77, 84, 92,
   125, 139, 148

Zengelis, Elia 61